ERRATUM

Page 111, second paragraph, should read:

The predominant requirement in Canada of obtaining leave to appeal to the Supreme Court of Canada has rendered that court inaccessible in all but the most important cases. Consequently that court is not necessarily available to correct error in intermediate appellate courts below. Indeed, it would appear that in considering whether leave will be granted, the fact that the members of the court hearing the application may disagree with the decision below, is by no means compelling.

Stare Decisis
in
Commonwealth
Appellate Courts

Stare Decisis in Commonwealth Appellate Courts

J. David Murphy
and
Robert Rueter

BUTTERWORTHS
Toronto

Stare Decisis in Commonwealth Appellate Courts
© 1981 Butterworth & Co. (Canada) Ltd.

Printed and bound in Canada

The Butterworth Group of Companies

Canada:
Butterworth & Co. (Canada) Ltd., Toronto and Vancouver

United Kingdom:
Butterworth & Co. (Publishers) Ltd., London

Australia:
Butterworths Pty. Ltd., Sydney

New Zealand:
Butterworths of New Zealand Ltd., Wellington

South Africa:
Butterworth & Co. (South Africa) Ltd., Durban

United States:
Butterworth (Publishers) Inc., Boston
Butterworth (Legal Publishers) Inc., Seattle
Mason Publishing Company, St. Paul

Canadian Cataloguing in Publication Data

б4978

Murphy, J. David.
  Stare decisis in Commonwealth appellate courts

Includes index.
ISBN 0-409-85373-9

1. Stare decisis — Commonwealth of Nations.
2. Appellate courts — Commonwealth of Nations.
I. Rueter, Robert.   II. Title.

K574.M87   347'.03   C81-094555-X

Preface

Among the world's legal systems, the common law is unique in acknowledging the binding effect of precedent. This doctrine which is described as the rule of *stare decisis* is not immutable. Recent events have focused attention on both the extent and the limits of its operation.

Courts of last resort, such as the House of Lords and the Supreme Court of Canada, no longer consider themselves bound by the rule. The extent of its operation in other courts, particularly intermediate courts of appeal, has become an important subject of inquiry. This is so especially in Canada where the abolition of appeals as of right to the Supreme Court of Canada has had the effect of making the decisions of provincial courts of appeal final in all but the most exceptional cases.

Because of these developments, publication of this study is both timely and important. The authors, who were law clerks with the Court of Appeal for Ontario, illuminate the subject with their special interest, knowledge and experience. This careful review of the operation of the rule of *stare decisis* in Canadian and other Commonwealth courts and the consideration of academic comment on it will be of immense benefit to both the Bench and the Bar.

The Honourable Mr. Justice Blair

Ontario Court of Appeal
Osgoode Hall
Toronto, Ontario
July, 1981

Acknowledgments

The authors and publishers of these articles have been most generous in giving permission for the reproduction in this text of work already in print. References, of course, appear where necessary and possible in the text. It is convenient for us to list below, for the assistance of the reader, the publishers and, in several instances, the authors for whose courtesy we are most grateful.

Every effort has been made to contact authors and publishers to obtain permissions. If the publisher is made aware of any errors which may have been made in obtaining permissions, the publisher will take steps to ensure that proper credit be given at that time.

Canadian Bar Review	W. Friedmann, "*Stare Decisis* at Common Law and under the Civil Code of Quebec" (1953), 31 Can. Bar Rev. 723.
	Daniel A. Lapres, "Comment" (1977), 55 Can. Bar Rev. 132.
	B. Laskin, "The Supreme Court of Canada: A Final Court of and for Canadians" (1951), 29 Can. Bar Rev. 1038.
	C.M. Schmitthoff, "The Growing Ambit of the Common Law" (1952), 30 Can. Bar Rev. 48.
Chitty's Law Journal	E.M. Hall, "Law Reform and the Judiciary's Role" (1972), 20 Chitty's L.J. 77.
Columbia Law Review	Douglas, "Stare Decisis" (1949), Colum. L. Rev. 735.

Lord Diplock	"The Courts as Legislators", an address delivered at The University of Birmingham, Holdsworth Club, March 26, 1965, pp. 18, 20, 21.
Israel Law Review Assoc.	B. Laskin, "The Institutional Character of the Judge" (1972), 7 Israel L. Rev. 329.
The Law Society of Upper Canada and Richard De Boo Ltd.	B. Dickson, "The Role and Function of Judges", The Law Society of Upper Canada Gazette (1980), Vol. XIV, p. 138.
Stevens & Sons Ltd.	F.J. Odgers, "Comment" (1976), 92 L.Q. Rev. 321.
Yale Law Journal Co.	E. Pound, "Liberty of Contract". Reprinted by permission of The Yale Law Journal Co. and Fred B. Rothman & Co. from The Yale Law Journal, Vol. 18, p. 464.

Table of Contents

Table of Cases

Chapter 1

Introduction

[The many-faceted doctrine of abiding by precedent, or the doctrine of *stare decisis,* is one of the pillars of the English system of law. This study examines one particular aspect of this doctrine, namely, the extent to which appellate courts regard themselves bound by their own previous decisions.] The study will concentrate on appellate courts in Canada, England and other Commonwealth jurisdictions, and will be concerned primarily with the application of *stare decisis* in civil, rather than criminal, cases.

The study attempts to provide a comprehensive picture of the current attitudes of Commonwealth appellate courts to the doctrine of *stare decisis.* This is perhaps its most important function. In addition, later sections focus on what might loosely be termed the 'rationale' for the rule — the arguments for and against its application in contemporary legal systems.] Also included is a treatment of several "collateral issues" or questions subsidiary to the main theme, such as the binding effect of decisions of different-sized panels.

[It is felt that this study of contemporary judicial attitudes toward *stare decisis* is particularly timely in an era when there are indications of stress within courts and clear signs that old rules are being reconsidered.] As will be seen in more detail *infra,* only a few appellate courts in the Commonwealth remain as the last bastions of *stare decisis.* [The relevance of the doctrine has been called into question in view of changing economic and social conditions, the trend toward limiting the right of appeal to higher appellate courts, and the lack of formal mechanisms by which intermediate appellate courts can bring questionable

---

[1] Throughout this study, the term *"stare decisis"* will be used in this somewhat limited sense. It is recognized that the term has broader connotations in other contexts.

1

precedents to the attention of higher courts.[2] These and other reasons for questioning the validity of the doctrine may not necessarily be determinative or even valid, but they are sufficient to justify an inquiry into the need for a rule which binds appellate courts to their previous decisions.

At common law there was no rule of law establishing the principle of *stare decisis*. Rather, there was a principle of courtesy among judges of co-ordinate authority, "a rule of etiquette or conventional decorum"[3] that they would defer to the opinions of one another when determinative of the question then decided, in the interests of certainty, stability and propriety in the law. One commentator has characterized the principle as "a constitutional rule binding in a constitutional sense."[4] In what has become a classic statement of the nature of the rule, Brett M.R. stated in *The Vera Cruz (No. 2)*:[5]

> It was the custom for each of the courts in Westminster Hall to hold itself bound by a previous decision of itself or of a court of co-ordinate jurisdiction, but there is no statute or common law rule by which one court is bound to abide by the decision of another of equal rank. It does so simply from what may be called the comity among judges. There is no common law or statutory rule to oblige a court to bow to its own decisions; it does so again on the grounds of judicial comity.

Similarly Brown J. observed in *Mast, Foos & Co. v. Stover Mfg. Co.*,[6] that:

> Comity is not a rule of law, but one of practice, convenience and expediency. It is something more than mere courtesy, which implies only deference to the opinion of others, since it has a substantial value in securing uniformity of decision, and discouraging repeated litigation of the same question. But its obligation is not imperative. If it were, the indiscreet action of one court might become a precedent, increasing in weight with each successive adjudication, until the whole country was tied down to an unsound principle. Comity persuades; but it does not command. It declares not how a case shall be decided, but how it may with propriety be decided. It recognizes the fact that the primary duty of every court is to dispose of cases according to the law and the facts; in

---

[2] Contrast this situation with the procedure available to a High Court judge in Ontario, for example, by virtue of s. 35 of The Judicature Act, R.S.O. 1970, c. 228.

[3] *Marconi Wireless Telegraph Co. of Canada v. Canadian Car & Foundry Co.* (1918), 44 D.L.R. 378, per Audette J. at p. 379.

[4] P.B. Kavanagh, "Stare Decisis in the House of Lords" (1973), 5 N.Z.U.L.R. 323 at p. 326.

[5] (1884), 9 P.D. 96 at p. 98.

[6] 177 U.S. 485 at p. 488 (7th cir., 1900).

a word, to decide them right. In doing so, the judge is bound to determine them according to his own convictions. If he can be clear in those convictions, he should follow them. It is only in cases where, in his own mind, there may be a doubt as to the soundness of his views that comity comes in play and suggests a uniformity of ruling to avoid confusion, until a higher court has settled the law.

[*Stare decisis* is of course a doctrine peculiar to the English common law; it is not found in civil law systems or in international law.[7]]

[In considering *stare decisis*, one must appreciate the vital distinction between a court being influenced by a prior decision ("paying it the utmost respect," etc.), and being bound by it. Prior to the mid- or late nineteenth century, judges in England did not regard themselves bound by earlier decisions, especially when these could be characterized as "absurd," "unreasonable," or "unjust."]Indicative of the then prevailing attitude is Lord Brougham's comment in *Birtwhistle v. Vardill*[8] that judges "in deciding important questions, should adopt the course, when they have gone wrong, of at once, in an open and manly way, retracing their steps, rather than persist in their error."

[The principle that superior courts are bound by their own previous decisions is of comparatively recent origin.] Lord Halsbury's claim in *London Tramways Co. v. London County Council*[9] that the rule of irreversible precedent had been "established now for some centuries" has been widely refuted. The *London Tramways* case itself is usually regarded as the beginning of the second phase in the history of *stare decisis* in England, i.e., the period of absolutism in the late nineteenth and early twentieth centuries. Actually, the notion that precedents are of binding effect probably originated somewhat earlier, in *Beamish v. Beamish.*[10]

The philosophical influence in the United States, which contributed in part to a shift from the "positivist" toward the "realist" end of the continuum in common-law jurisdictions in the middle decades of this century, must be noted here.[11]

---

[7] See *Trendex Trading Corporation Ltd. v. Central Bank of Nigeria,* [1977] 1 All E.R. 881 (C.A.). See also Article 59 of the Statute of the Court of International Justice.

[8] (1840), 7 Cl. & Fin. 895 at p. 922. For an interesting commentary on this era, see R. Cross, "Blackstone v. Bentham" (1976), 92 L.Q.R. 516 at pp. 518-520.

[9] [1898] A.C. 375 at p. 379.

[10] (1861), 9 H.L. Cas. 274.

[11] See P.B. Kavanagh, op. cit., at p. 323 ff.

In the early part of the twentieth century, Pound[12] observed that:

> Jurisprudence is the last in the march of the sciences away from the method of deduction from predetermined conceptions. The sociological movement in jurisprudence, the movement for pragmatism as a philosophy of law, the movement for the adjustment of principles and doctrines to the human conditions they are to govern rather than to assumed first principles, the movement for putting the human factor in the central place and relegating logic to its true position as an instrument, has scarcely shown itself as yet in America.

However, it was the American courts which led the "movement" toward breaking down the strictures of *stare decisis.* They seemed able to pursue a safe course between the extremes of a never and an ever changing law.

It is far too easy to view *stare decisis* in terms of black or white. Many commentators argue for a complete abolition of the doctrine which itself is often incorrectly assumed to be absolute in nature. One must not overlook the manifold of intermediate positions which stand between complete abolition and rigid adherence. These would include prospective overruling, the giving of notice of possible future changes, relevant procedural changes, the use of guidelines in policy statements and the delineation of certain areas in which *stare decisis* is most appropriate. Accordingly, these possibilities will be examined in later sections of this study.

---

[12] E. Pound, "Liberty of Contract" reprinted by permission of the Yale Law Journal Company and Fred B. Rothman & Co. from The Yale Law Journal.

Chapter 2

Stare Decisis in English Appellate Courts

The attitude of English appellate courts toward the doctrine of *stare decisis* is an important factor to be considered by Canadian courts, if for no other reason than that the Canadian system of law has its roots in England. The following paragraphs will focus on the position taken by the various English appellate courts, with particular emphasis on the most recent statements.[1]

House of Lords

In *London Tramways Co. v. London County Council,*[2] Halsbury L.C. made what was perhaps the most momentous early statement of the effect of the doctrine of *stare decisis:* "A decision of this House once given upon a point of law is conclusive, upon this House afterwards, and . . . it is impossible to raise that question again . . . [N]othing but an Act of Parliament can set right that which is alleged to be wrong in a judgment of this House."[3] The early view was that House of Lords decisions were themselves in the nature of legislation.[4]

This approach was strictly adhered to in the following decades. For example, in *Admiralty Commissioners v. Valverda*[5] Lord Wright noted that while the House of Lords had power to overrule even a long

---

[1] The Judicial Committee will not be considered in this list of English Courts. It seems clear that the Privy Council "has never countenanced the doctrine that its own decisions are not reviewable": *Australian Agricultural Co. v. Federated Engine Drivers and Firemen's Association of Australasia* (1913), 17 C.L.R. 261; *Tooth v. Power,* [1891] A.C. 284; *Attorney-General for Ontario v. Canada Temperance Federation,* [1946] A.C. 193 at p. 206; *Baker v. The Queen,* [1975] A.C. 774 at pp,787-88; Cross, *Precedent in English Law,* p. 105.

[2] [1898] A.C. 375.

[3] *Ibid.* at p. 379.

[4] See a discussion of this in *Australian Agricultural Co. v. Federated Engine Drivers and Firemen's Association of Australasia,* op. cit., f.n.1, at pp. 274-5; see also "The Role of a Final Appeal Court in a Democracy: The House of Lords Today", 48 Mod. L.R. 509.

[5] [1938] A.C. 173 at pp. 194-5 (emphasis added).

established course of decisions, *provided it had not itself determined the question*, it would in general adopt this course only in plain cases where serious inconvenience or injustice would follow from perpetuating an erroneous construction or ruling of law. In *London Transport Executive v. Betts*,[6] Lord Reid observed that:

> It has long been established practice that any decision of this House in a previous case on a question of law, such as the interpretation of a statute, shall be regarded as binding, and shall be followed, whether or not the question was adequately argued or considered, and however much your Lordships may disagree with the decision. I would not myself be against a modification of this strict practice, but so long as it exists I do not think I am entitled to depart from it.

Lord Denning,[7] however, did not agree with this approach and would have allowed "fundamental principle" to prevail over a "particular precedent."

In *Myers v. D.P.P.*[8] Lord Reid, while ostensibly supporting the doctrine of *stare decisis*, gave some hints of what was to come:

> I have never taken a narrow view of the functions of this House as an appellate tribunal. The common law must be developed to meet changing economic conditions and habits of thought, and I would not be deterred by expressions of opinion in this House in old cases. But there are limits to what we can or should do. If we are to extend the law it must be by the development and application of fundamental principles. We cannot introduce arbitrary conditions or limitations: that must be left to legislation. And if we do in effect change the law, we ought in my opinion only to do that in cases where our decision will produce some finality or certainty.

The well-known *Practice Statement*[9] read by Lord Gardiner L.C. on behalf of the Lords on July 26, 1966 signalled an apparent change in attitude. Its full text is as follows:

> Their Lordships regard the use of precedent as an indispensable foundation upon which to decide what is the law and its application to individual cases. It provides at least some degree of certainty upon which individuals can rely in the conduct of their affairs, as well as a basis for orderly development of legal rules.

---

6 [1959] A.C. 213 at p. 232.
7 *Ibid.* at pp. 246-7.
8 [1965] A.C. 1001 at p. 1021.
9 *Practice Statement (Judicial Precedent)*, [1966] 1 W.L.R. 1234.

Their Lordships nevertheless recognise that too rigid adherence to precedent may lead to injustice in a particular case and also unduly restrict the proper development of the law. They propose, therefore, to modify their present practice and, while treating former decisions of this House as normally binding, to depart from a previous decision when it appears right to do so.

In this connection they will bear in mind the danger of disturbing retrospectively the basis on which contracts, settlements of property and fiscal arrangements have been entered into and also the special need for certainty as to the criminal law.

This announcement is not intended to affect the use of precedent elsewhere than in this House.

It is important to consider, first, the possible reasons for such an announcement at this time; second, statements contained in subsequent cases which serve to shed light on the meaning of the announcement; and, finally, the extent to which the new freedom of the *Practice Statement* has actually been exercised.

It would appear that the commentators are at a loss to explain exactly why the announcement was made in this form and at this time. Obviously there had been strong sentiment within the House of Lords which was not fully manifest in the cases. Lord Kilbrandon, Chairman of the Scottish Law Commission at the relevant time, has suggested[10] that the Lord Chancellor was influenced by the circulation of a draft Bill, which originated in Scotland, to the effect that the House of Lords would not be bound by its previous decisions. Lord Reid's explanation is found in *Jones v. Secretary of State for Social Services*:[11]

My understanding of the position when this resolution was adopted was and is that there were a comparatively small number of reported decisions of this House which were generally thought to be impeding the proper development of the law or to have led to results which were unjust or contrary to public policy and that such decisions should be reconsidered as opportunities arose.

In an interview in The Solicitors' Journal[12] soon after the *Practice Statement* was released, Lord Gardiner stated that the announcement meant that the House of Lords would depart

---

[10] *Note* (1967), 83 L.Q.R. 176. See also Jack A. Hiller, "The Law-Creative Role of Appellate Courts in the Commonwealth," (1978) 27 Int. & Comp. L.Q. 85, for a discussion of possible reasons behind the *Practice Statement*, as well as excellent treatments of other topics in the general area of precedent.

[11] [1972] A.C. 944 at p. 966.

[12] September 30, 1966, at p. 733.

from a prior decision when there would be "no repercussions."
Cases since 1966 have furnished somewhat fuller guidelines. In
Pettitt v. Pettitt[13] Lord Reid differentiated between cases
involving "lawyer's law" and those in areas of "public
controversy":

> We must first have in mind or decide how far it is proper for the
> courts to go in adapting or adding to existing law. Whatever views may
> have prevailed in the last century, I think that it is now widely
> recognised that it is proper for the courts in appropriate cases to develop
> or adapt existing rules of the common law to meet new conditions. I say
> in appropriate cases because I think we ought to recognise a difference
> between cases where we are dealing with "lawyer's law" and cases where
> we are dealing with matters which directly affect the lives and interests
> of large sections of the community and which raise issues which are the
> subject of public controversy and on which laymen are as well able to
> decide as are lawyers. On such matters it is not for the courts to proceed
> on their view of public policy for that would be to encroach on the
> province of Parliament.
>
> I would therefore refuse to consider whether property belonging to
> either spouse ought to be regarded as family property for that would be
> introducing a new conception into English law and not merely
> developing existing principles.

In *Cassell & Co. Ltd. v. Broome*[14] Lord Hailsham asserted
that the House of Lords, in assuming the powers adopted by the
Practice Statement, did not intend to "tear up the doctrine of
precedent." Significantly, the fact that *Rookes v. Barnard*,[15] the
well-known exemplary damages case, "was decided neither *per
incuriam* nor *ultra vires* this House," was still an important
element to be considered, in Lord Hailsham's view.

Jones v. Secretary of State for Social Services[16] provides some
useful insights into the Lords' perception of the *Practice
Statement. Jones* was not a case in which the House departed
from a previous decision. Of the full committee of seven Lords,
three thought the prior decision was right and four thought it
was wrong; however, one of the group of four was nevertheless of
the view that they should not depart from the decision.

---

[13] [1970] A.C. 777 at pp. 794-5.

[14] [1972] A.C. 1027 at p. 1083.

[15] [1964] A.C. 1129.

[16] [1972] A.C. 944. For a full discussion of all the speeches in this case, see J. Stone, "The Lords
at the Crossroads — When to 'Depart' and How" (1972), Aust. L.J. 483. See also L.V. Prott,
"When Will a Superior Court Overrule Its Own Decision?", (1978), 52 Aust. L.J. 304.

It is clear from the *Jones* case that a court must be unable to distinguish before it can overrule. However, it was felt that the old practice of evading decisions by fine distinctions promoted even further uncertainty. This theme pervades Lord Reid's view of the new power of the House of Lords:

> The old view was that any departure from rigid adherence to precedent would weaken . . . certainty. I did not and do not accept that view. It is notorious that where an existing decision is disapproved but cannot be overruled courts tend to distinguish it on inadequate grounds. I do not think that they act wrongly in so doing: they are adopting the less bad of the only alternatives open to them. But this is bound to lead to uncertainty for no one can say in advance whether in a particular case the court will or will not feel bound to follow the old unsatisfactory decision. On balance it seems to me that overruling such a decision will promote and not impair the certainty of the law.
>
> But that certainty will be impaired unless this practice is used sparingly. I would not seek to categorise cases in which it should or cases in which it should not be used. As time passes experience will supply some guide. But I would venture the opinion that the typical case for reconsidering an old decision is where some broad issue is involved, and that it should only be in rare cases that we should reconsider questions of construction of statutes or other documents.[17]

In deciding that the prior decision should not be reconsidered, Lord Reid was influenced by the fact that "no broad issue of justice or public policy . . . nor any question of legal principle" was involved. The issue, it was said, was simply the proper construction of provisions in a statute; any administrative difficulties caused by the prior decision could be remedied by statutory amendment. Viscount Dilhorne[18] stressed the certainty argument and asserted that the House should only refuse to follow a prior decision "in rare cases." However, when such cases arise and the prior decision is clearly wrong, it is "easier to decide that a recent case should not be followed than if it is one that has stood for a long time, for if it is in the latter category many may have acted in reliance on it." In contrast to Lord Reid (and Lord Wilberforce),[19] Viscount Dilhorne could see no valid reason why the House of Lords "should be especially reluctant to correct an error if the decision thought to be wrong is as to the construction of a statute".

---

[17] *Ibid.* at p. 966.
[18] *Ibid.* at p. 993.
[19] *Ibid.* at p. 995.

In *Knuller v. D.P.P.*[20] Lord Reid[21] asserted once again that the *Practice Statement* did not mean that the House was free to reverse a prior decision whenever it thought such a decision was wrong. Lord Morris[22] listed six reasons why in the instant appeal it was inappropriate to review the prior decision:

> . . . (1) The decision constituted a clear pronouncement of this House as to what the law was and had been; (2) It was a decision in relation to the criminal law where certainty is so desirable; (3) The decision has been acted upon and many criminal prosecutions have been based upon the authority of it; (4) The decision was one which attracted public attention and which on different occasions has been brought particularly to the attention of Parliament; (5) Parliament has not altered the law; (6) whether a change in the law could or could not have been effected as part of the provisions of the Obscene Publications Act 1964, or of the Sexual Offences Act 1967, or of the Theatres Act 1968, is immaterial. The provisions and contents of those Acts could well have stimulated an alteration of the law as laid down in *Shaw's* case had Parliament so desired.

In *Fitzleet Estates Ltd. v. Cherry*[23] the House of Lords refused to depart from an earlier decision involving an identical fact situation, on the bases that no material change in circumstances had been shown, no new arguments of law or fact could be advanced in addition to those put forth on the earlier occasion, and no manifest "injustice" flowed therefrom. The mere facts that the earlier decision might be regarded as having been wrongly decided, or that it had been decided by a narrow margin, were said to be insufficient in themselves.

In *Hesperides Hotels v. Muftizade*[24] the House of Lords refused to depart from an earlier rule (which had been subjected to considerable academic criticism over the years) on the basis that there was no change in circumstances sufficient to warrant a revision. Interestingly, the House of Lords seemed to be

---

[20] [1973] A.C. 435.

[21] *Ibid.* at p. 455.

[22] *Ibid.* at p. 466. While this study does not attempt to examine the doctrine of *stare decisis* in relation to criminal matters, it is worthwhile to note that at least one commentator has argued that the House of Lords has been much too cautious in its use of the new *Practice Statement* 'freedom' in the area of criminal law: see R. Brazier, "Overruling House of Lords Criminal Cases", [1973] Crim. L.R. 98.

[23] [1977] 3 All E.R. 996 (H.L.). The speeches in this case contain useful comments on the *Practice Statement.* See also A.N. Khan, "Unprecedented Judicial Precedents" (1978), 122 Sol. J. 702, 721.

[24] [1978] 3 W.L.R. 378 (H.L.).

influenced in part by the fact that the rule still prevailed in other common law jurisdictions.

Since the *Practice Statement* in 1966 it would appear that the House of Lords has only overruled itself on three occasions. (*Conway v. Rimmer*[25] is a questionable fourth case in which the House of Lords swept away *Duncan v. Cammell, Laird,*[26] arguably without "departing from it." However, only Lord Morris[27] unequivocally abandoned the *Duncan* case.)

British Railways Board v. Herrington,[28] involved a child trespasser on a railway. There the House of Lords clearly departed from a 1929 case of its own in which it asserted the rigid rule denying recovery to trespassers. Lord Reid[29] departed from the earlier case on the basis of changed "public policy," despite the fact that Parliament had legislated in the occupiers' liability area in the meantime without changing this aspect of the law. Lord Pearson[30] felt that the prior decision had been "rendered obsolete by changes in physical and social conditions" and had become "an incumbrance impeding the proper development of the law": the old law was "plainly inadequate for modern conditions, and its rigid and restrictive character has impeded the proper development of the common law in this field." Lord Diplock[31] felt that the freedom derived from the *Practice Statement* allowed the House of Lords to depart from the prior decision rather than having to resort to such "fictions" as imputing a "licence" in occupiers' liability cases.

The Johanna Oldendorff[32] involved a question of shipping law. A rule established by the House of Lords thirteen years earlier was abandoned for reasons given by Lord Reid:[33]

> A main objective of the law should be that it should appear sensible and easy of application by those whose affairs it governs. I would not think it sufficient to justify our intervention that the criterion approved in *The Aello* is illogical but if in addition we find that it causes uncertainty in practice then I think that we ought to intervene.

---

[25] [1968] 1 All E.R. 874. See J. Stone's note on this case in (1969), 69 Col. L.R. 1162, 1171, for an exhaustive treatment of the approaches taken in the various speeches.

[26] [1942] A.C. 624.

[27] [1968] 1 All E.R. 874 at p. 892.

[28] [1972] 1 All E.R. 749.

[29] *Ibid.* at p. 757.

[30] *Ibid.* at pp. 785-6.

[31] *Ibid.* at p. 790.

[32] [1973] 3 All E.R. 148.

[33] *Ibid.* at p. 155.

Miliangos v. George Frank (Textiles) Ltd.[34] deals with several aspects of the doctrine of *stare decisis* and will be referred to in other parts of this study. Here the House of Lords clearly relied on the *Practice Statement* to justify a departure from an earlier decision outlining a rule of conversion in situations where English judgments were obtained for foreign debts in foreign currency. It was held that the instability which had overtaken the pound sterling and other major currencies since the earlier House of Lords decision, as well as the procedures evolved in consequence by the English courts and by arbitrators in the City of London to secure payment of foreign currency debts in foreign currency, justified a departure from that decision since the introduction of a new and more satisfactory rule would enable the courts to keep pace with commercial needs without undue practical and procedural difficulties.

English Court of Appeal

The leading case of *Young v. Bristol Aeroplane Company, Limited*[35] left little doubt that, subject to certain exceptions, the Court of Appeal is bound by its previous decisions. Earlier cases had suggested that the Court of Appeal would not always be bound. In *Re South Durham Iron Company*,[36] Baggallay L.J.[37] seemed to suggest that the Court could depart from prior decisions in circumstances not limited to *per incuriam* situations:

> . . . the answer generally would certainly be that the Court as now constituted is bound by the previous decisions of the same Court. But I am far from saying that there are not exceptional circumstances under which the Court would not necessarily be so bound. I may mention, by way of illustration, a case in which a decision has been very recent, and the circumstances connected with it show that it was not very fully considered. Again, where doubts are entertained by one or more of the Judges who had taken part in such decision; and thirdly, though more rarely, where there is a concurrence of opinion, outside the members of

---

[34] [1975] 3 W.L.R. 758. See comments on this case by D.A. Lapres in (1977), 55 C.B. Rev. 132; B. Elkan in (1976) 120 Sol. J. 446; and I. Ramsay in (1977) 15 U.W.O. L. Rev. 213.

[35] [1944] 1 K.B. 718, affd. [1946] A.C. 163. There is authority to the effect that the Court of Appeal also considers itself bound by decisions of older courts of coordinate jurisdiction, such as the Exchequer Chamber: See *Hanau v. Ehrlich*, [1911] 2 K.B. 1056, *R. v. Taylor*, [1950] 2 K.B. 368. For an interesting discussion of this question in another geographical context, see A.D. Burgess, "Judicial Precedent in the West Indies", (1978) 7 Anglo-Amer. L. Rev. 113.

[36] (1879), 11 Ch. D. 579.

[37] *Ibid.* at p. 593.

the Court so constituted, to the effect that the decision was one which could not be supported . . .

Bramwell L.J.[38] made it clear that he would not go this far.

The judgment of Greer L.J. in *Re Shoesmith*[39] contains a startling proposition:

> the Court has more than once, sitting as a Court with all its six members, decided that it can overrule a decision of the Court of Appeal which has held the field for a number of years. If the Court of Appeal, sitting with its six members, can do so, *equally a Court sitting with a quorum of members can do the same thing.* Although, as a matter of courtesy and of usual practice, this Court deems it right to follow its own decisions in earlier cases, there is no rule of law which compels it to do so.

Slesser L.J.[40] agreed with this view. It should be noted, however, that this case dealt with a narrow point involving the Court's own procedure; furthermore, the prior cases in question may well have been decided *per incuriam.*

Young v. Bristol Aeroplane Company, Limited,[41] according to Professor Goodhart,[42] represented the "high water mark of absolutism." Lord Greene M.R., speaking for the full court, asserted that the doctrine of *stare decisis* was "beyond controversy." The Court of Appeal is bound to follow its own decisions and those of courts of co-ordinate jurisdiction and the full court is in the same position in this respect as a division of the court consisting of three members. The only exceptions to this rule are, according to *Young,* (1) the court is entitled and bound to decide which of two conflicting decisions of its own it will follow; (2) the court is bound to refuse to follow a decision of its own which, though not expressly overruled, cannot, in its opinion, stand with a decision of the House of Lords; and (3) the court is not bound to follow a decision of its own if it is satisfied that the decision was given per incuriam, e.g., where a statute or a rule having statutory effect would have affected the decision but was not brought to the attention of the earlier court.

One commentator[43] has argued that the decision in *Young* is

---

[38] *Ibid.* at p. 596.

[39] [1938] 2 K.B. 637 at p. 644 (emphasis added).

[40] *Ibid.* at p. 645.

[41] [1944] 1 K.B. 718, affd. [1946] A.C. 163.

[42] "Precedents in the Court of Appeal" (1947), 9 Camb. L.J. 349. See also C.E.F. Rickett, "Precedent in the Court of Appeal" (1980) 43 Mod. L.R. 136.

[43] C.M. Schmitthoff, "The Growing Ambit of the Common Law" (1952), 30 C.B. Rev. 48.

"janus-faced; it extended the absolute rule of precedent by laying down that the Court of Appeal is bound by its own decisions, and, at the same time, formulated the exceptions to that rule so widely that the courts, in subsequent decisions, were able to qualify the strict rule considerably." Other commentators[44] have argued that the exceptions destroy the certainty and uniformity on which the main rule is supposedly founded.

The *Young* case has been followed in a large number of Court of Appeal decisions in recent years.[45] The Court in *Williams v. Glasbrook Brothers, Ltd.*[46] went so far as to hold that even if the Court of Appeal had misinterpreted a previous decision of the House of Lords, such a misinterpretation would not justify a later Court of Appeal in refusing to follow the earlier decision of that court.

The debate in the last decade has centered around Lord Denning's attempt to persuade his brethren that the Court of Appeal should follow the House of Lords' lead and refuse to be strictly bound by previous decisions. In *Gallie v. Lee*[47] Lord Denning M.R. failed to convince Russell[48] and Salmon L.JJ.[49] Russell L.J. stressed the desirability of certainty and the availability of the House of Lords to correct the errors of the Court of Appeal. Salmon L.J. regarded as undesirable the present practice, which "apparently rests solely upon a concept of judicial comity laid down many years ago and automatically followed ever since." However he was of the view that a pronouncement of the whole court was necessary to "effectively alter a practice which [was] so deeply rooted."

In *R. v. Newsome*[50] Widgery L.J. remarked that "there is discernible [in the authorities] a slight tendency in the civil division of this court to relax the fetters of the doctrine," but that developments "have certainly not reached the point at which it would be appropriate for us to regard them as in any sense binding upon us."

---

[44] See, for example, Goodhart, op. cit., f.n. 40.

[45] It was also recently endorsed by the House of Lords in *Miliangos v. Geo. Frank (Textiles) Ltd.*, [1975] 3 W.L.R. 758.

[46] [1947] 2 All E.R. 884.

[47] [1969] 2 W.L.R. 901.

[48] *Ibid.* at p. 918.

[49] *Ibid.* at p. 925.

[50] [1970] 2 Q.B. 711 at p. 716.

In *Tiverton Estates Ltd. v. Wearwell Ltd.*[51] Lord Denning[52] was willing to concede that his view of *stare decisis* in the Court of Appeal had not received wide acceptance in the Court. However, in this case he was able to accomplish his purpose by seizing upon the "choice of conflicting decisions" exception in the *Young* rule. Stamp[53] and Scarman[54] L.JJ. asserted that they remained among the "unpersuaded brethren" of Lord Denning M.R., Scarman L.J. remarking that the Court of Appeal was "better without" any new freedom.

In *Carr v. Carr*[55] the Court of Appeal had occasion to consider a previous decision of its own in which, it was argued, one side had not been heard and there was a possibility that a provision of a statute had been overlooked. The Court refused to hold that the prior decision had been decided *per incuriam*, and followed it *dubitante,* expressing the hope that the matter would soon come before the House of Lords.

In *Farrell v. Alexander*[56] Lord Denning M.R. refused to follow a previous decision on the grounds that it was "wrongly decided. So much so that I do not think it is binding on us", and that the result of an appeal to the House of Lords would be "a foregone conclusion." Lawton and Scarman L.JJ did not endorse his approach, though the latter seemed to hold some sympathy for Lord Denning's view. The *Young* rule was approved once again in the House of Lords, where the decision of the Court of Appeal was reversed. Lord Simon in *Farrell v. Alexander,*[57] noted that:

> . . . The Court of Appeal occupies a crucial position in one judicial system. Most appeals stop there. It handles an immense volume of business. It sits in a number of divisions. Unless it follows its own decisions, as the law directs, litigation will be a gamble on which

---

[51] [1974] 2 W.L.R. 176.

[52] *Ibid.* at p. 185. For a somewhat similar "concession" see Lord Denning M.R. in *Miliangos v. George Frank (Textiles) Ltd.,* [1975] 1 All E.R. 1076 at p. 1085 (C.A.).

[53] *Ibid.* at p. 194.

[54] *Ibid.* at pp. 195-6.

[55] [1974] 1 All E.R. 1193.

[56] [1976] 1 All E.R. 129, reversed [1976] 2 All E.R. 721 (H.L.). See comments on this case by A.S. Owen in (1977), 40 Mod. L.R. 216, and by F.J. Odgers in (1976), 92 L.Q.R. 321. The latter commentator suggests at p. 323 that a full court of the Court of Appeal should have power to overrule its own decisions: "There might be a discretion in the Court of Appeal either to grant leave to appeal to the House of Lords or, at less cost to the parties, to have the appeal re-argued before a full court with power to overrule its own decisions. The last would be at the risk of the respondent, if ultimately unsuccessful, obtaining leave to appeal from the Lords though this would appear unlikely".

[57] [1976] 2 All E.R. 721 at p. 742. See also *Harnett v. Harnett,* [1974] 1 W.L.R. 219.

division of the court is to handle the appeal and what law will be declared there.

While recent judicial pronouncements may suggest that *Young* stands unassailed, it is worth noting a recent trend toward creating further exceptions to the broad rule in the case. One respected commentator[58] has described *Boys v. Chaplin*[59] as illustrative of a trend in the Court of Appeal to "graft exceptions onto the general rule of *stare decisis* as far as its own decisions are concerned." In this case a court composed of Lord Denning M.R., Lord Upjohn, and Diplock L.J. held that the full Court of Appeal is not precluded by its own rule of *stare decisis* in respect of final decisions from overruling an interlocutory decision of two lords justice which the court considers to be wrong.

In *Worcester Works Finance Ltd. v. Cooden Engineering Co. Ltd.*,[60] a case that evidently escaped the notice of the commentators, the Court of Appeal effectively carved out another exception to the *Young* rule. In this case all members of the Court (Lord Denning M.R., Phillimore and Megaw L.JJ.) regarded themselves at liberty to depart from previous decisions of the Court of Appeal which had subsequently been overruled by the Privy Council, despite the fact that the Court of Appeal did not regard itself as bound by decisions of the Privy Council.

Despite statements in recent Court of Appeal and House of Lords decisions to the effect that the Court is bound by its previous decisions (except in the case of the exceptions enunciated in *Young*), it is clear that the Court, in two recent instances, has refused to follow its past decisions because of a change in social mores. In *Cooke v. Head*[61] the Court dealt with the question of apportionment of beneficial interests in a "matrimonial home" when the parties are unmarried. Lord Denning M.R., Karminski and Orr L.JJ. apportioned the interests "broadly, just as we do in husband and wife cases," and declined to follow an earlier case which, for purposes of apportionment, treated a mistress as being in a different position from a wife.

In *Dyson Holdings Ltd. v. Fox*[62] a Court of Appeal composed

---

[58] Rupert Cross, "Recent Developments in the Practice of Precedent — The Triumph of Common Sense" (1969), 43 Aust. L.J. 3. See also J. Stone, "A Court of Appeal in Search of Itself: Thoughts on Judges' Liberation" (1971), 71 Col. L.R. 1420.

[59] [1968] 2 Q.B. 1.

[60] [1971] 3 All E.R. 708.

[61] [1972] 2 All E.R. 38.

[62] [1975] 3 All E.R. 1030.

of Lord Denning M.R., James and Bridge L.JJ. refused to follow a decision of the Court in which, for purposes of rent legislation, common-law partners had been held not to be members of the same family. Lord Denning M.R.,[63] who did not distinguish the two cases although it might have been possible to do so, was of the view that the Court would not be bound "when, owing to the lapse of time, and the change in social conditions, the previous decision is not in accord with modern thinking." He stated that, alternatively, the prior decision was wrongly decided from the standpoint of statutory interpretation. James L.J.[64] apparently felt that the earlier case was a binding authority, but only as to the meaning of "family" at that time. In his view "the word 'family' must be given its popular meaning at the time relevant to the decision in the particular case." It is difficult to see how this can be anything but a rejection of the earlier decision. Bridge L.J.[65] felt that if language can change its meaning to accord with changing social attitudes, then a decision on the meaning of a word in a statute should not continue to bind after such a change.

In addition, the recent case of *Davis v. Johnson*,[66] heard by a five-member court, contains Lord Denning's[67] strongest judgment yet in support of the proposition that the Court of Appeal is not bound by its previous decisions. In this case he was of the view that the Court should adopt, where one of its earlier decisions is clearly wrong, guidelines similar to those adopted by the House of Lords in the 1966 *Practice Statement*. Alternatively, the Court should regard this situation as another exception to those stated in the *Young* case: "the list of exceptions . . . is now getting so large that they are in the process of eating up the rule itself." Sir George Baker P.[68] agreed that the Court of Appeal should not regard itself as bound by decisions that they thought were clearly wrong. Shaw L.J.[69] appeared to agree with Lord Denning M.R. and Baker P. Goff L.J.,[70] with whom Cumming-Bruce L.J.[71] agreed, held that he was bound by the previous decisions of the Court, and that a

---

[63] *Ibid.* at p. 1033.
[64] *Ibid.* at p. 1035.
[65] *Ibid.* at p. 1036.
[66] [1978] 2 W.L.R. 182.
[67] *Ibid.* at pp. 193 *ff.*
[68] *Ibid.* at pp. 204 *ff.*
[69] *Ibid.* at pp. 220 *ff.*
[70] *Ibid.* at pp. 206 *ff.*
[71] *Ibid.* at pp. 222 *ff.*

Court of five judges was just as much bound as a Court of three judges.

The views of the majority of the Court of Appeal in *Davis v. Johnson* on the place of *stare decisis* in that Court were severely attacked by the House of Lords,[72] led by Lord Diplock. In the latter's words, "this House should take this occasion to re-affirm expressly, unequivocally and unanimously that the rule laid down in the *Bristol Aeroplane* case as to *stare decisis* is still binding on the Court of Appeal." A question is raised as to the propriety of the higher court commenting on the role of *stare decisis* in the intermediate court. There would seem to be a conceptual difficulty in this regard, as the higher court's sole concern ought merely to be the correctness of the decision on the merits.[73]

English Divisional Court[74]

The modern view is that the Divisional Court is bound by its own decisions, whether or not there exists an appeal to the Court of Appeal.[75] However, when a Divisional Court is faced with conflicting decisions it is free to decide which to follow.[76] Where there is a decision of two judges and one of three, the rule is to respect the decision of the court of three judges,[77] though it has been said that "a Divisional Court of five judges has no greater powers than one of three or even two."[78]

---

[72] [1978] 1 All E.R. 1132 (H.L.). See comments in D. Bradley (1978), 41 Mod. L. Rev. 592; P.V. Baker (1978), 94 L.Q.R. 358; D. Lasok (1978), 128 New L.J. 124, 539; and R. Brownsword and M. Hayes (1978), 29 No. Ire. L.Q. 296.

[73] See *Attorney-General of Saint Christopher, Nevis and Anguilla v. Reynolds*, [1979] 3 All E.R. 129 in which the Judicial Committee of the Privy Council commented on the propriety of the West Indies Associated States Court of Appeal considering itself to be bound by its prior decisions. But Lord Salmon added (at pp. 139-49): "The opinion of their Lordships' Board and of the House of Lords [on the question of an intermediate appellate court being bound by its prior decisions] can . . . be only of persuasive authority. No doubt it would be treated with great respect but it cannot be of binding authority because the point can never come before this Board or the House of Lords for decision. Indeed if a case came before either in which the Court of Appeal had refused to follow one of its own previous decisions on a point of law the appeal would have to be dismissed if the final appellate tribunal concluded that the previous decision was wrong."

[74] See O.M. Stone, "Stare Decisis in the Divisional Court" (1951), 14 Mod. L.R. 219.

[75] *Police Authority for Huddersfield v. Watson*, [1947] K.B. 842. There is authority to the effect that mere *dicta* expressed unanimously by the three judges of a Divisional Court ought to be applied by the judges of another Divisional Court: *Mills v. L.C.C.*, [1925] 1 K.B. 213.

[76] *Ratkinsky v. Jacobs*, [1929] 1 K.B. 24.

[77] *De Vries v. Smallridge*, [1928] 1 K.B. 482.

[78] *Younghusband v. Luftig*, [1949] 2 K.B. 354.

Chapter 3

Stare Decisis in Canadian Appellate Courts

The Supreme Court of Canada

In Canada, as in other common law jurisdictions, judicial attitudes respecting the doctrine of *stare decisis* have undergone considerable change. This is particularly so in the years following the pronouncement of the House of Lords that it would no longer consider itself necessarily bound by its previous decisions.

An examination of the Canadian position must commence with the Supreme Court decision in *Stuart v. The Bank of Montreal.*[1] Prior thereto it was generally considered that previous decisions were binding, although the proposition was not entirely free from doubt.[2] The *Stuart* case, at least as subsequently interpreted, settled the matter for many years. The statement of Duff J., with whose judgment Fitzpatrick C.J. concurred, is most frequently quoted as outlining the Canadian rule. He stated:

> Some question is raised, whether or not we are entitled to disregard a previous decision of this court laying down a substantive rule of law. This court is, of course, not a court of final resort in the sense in which the House of Lords is because our decisions are reviewable by the Privy Council; but only in very exceptional circumstances would the Court of Exchequer Chamber or the Lords Justices, sitting in appeal, (from which courts there was an appeal as of right to the House of Lords), have felt themselves at liberty to depart from one of their own previous decisions. That is also the principle upon which the Court of Appeal

---

[1] (1909), 41 S.C.R. 516, aff'd [1911] A.C. 120.
[2] *Ibid.* per Anglin J. at pp. 541-544.

now acts; . . . and the Court of Appeal, in any province where the basis
of the law is the common law of England, would act upon the same
view. Quite apart from this, there are, I think, considerations of public
convenience too obvious to require statement which make it our duty to
apply this principle to the decisions of this court. What exceptional
circumstances would justify a departure from the general rule, we need
not consider; because there was, in the circumstances in which *Cox v.
Adams* was decided, nothing in the least degree exceptional.[3]

After a very careful review of the relevant authorities, Anglin J.
observed:

The Supreme Court of Canada occupies a somewhat peculiar position.
From it no appeal lies as of right. By special leave an appeal may be had
to the Judicial Committee. In a great majority of cases which it hears it
is a final appellate tribunal; in other cases, it occupies the position of an
intermediate appellate court. But, whether it be regarded as final or
intermediate, in view of the current of recent decisions to which
reference has been made, the attitude of this court towards its previous
decisions upon questions of law should, in my opinion, be the same . . .
[W]e should not, in my opinion, hesitate now to determine that, . . .
unless perhaps in very exceptional circumstances, a previous deliberate
and definite decision of this court will be held binding, if it is clear that
it was not the result of some mere slip or inadvertence. . .

[I]t is of supreme importance that people may know with certainty
what the law is, and this end can only be attained by a loyal adherence
to the doctrine of *stare decisis*. I see no good reason why this doctrine
should not be applied, and many very cogent reasons why it should
prevail in this court.[4]

Davies J. simply stated that the previous decision was binding[5]
while Idington J. (dissenting) was of the opinion that since there
was no concurrence of opinion in the majority as to the
application of a principle of law in the previous decision, it was
not binding upon him.[6]
Of the two judges in *Stuart* who fully considered the extent to
which *stare decisis* applied, both allowed that "very exceptional
circumstances" might constitute an exception to the rule.
Neither ventured an opinion as to what exceptional
circumstances might justify a departure, although in the view of

[3] *Ibid.* at p. 535.
[4] *Ibid.* at pp. 548-550.
[5] *Ibid.* at p. 526.
[6] *Ibid.* at pp. 527, 529-30.

Anglin J., they would involve something other than "some mere slip or inadvertence."

The principle remained unchanged for over half a century, the *Stuart* case frequently being cited by the Supreme Court as having settled the question.[7] It is of interest, however, to note that in *Peters v. Perras,*[8] a unanimous judgment of the court delivered by Fitzpatrick C.J. some six months after the *Stuart* case was heard, the Supreme Court overruled its previous decision of a year and a half in *The Union Investment Co. v. Wells.*[9] The court delivered brief reasons and did not refer to the *Union Investment* case; however, it did refer to an Ontario High Court decision which had referred to that case. The court that decided *Peters v. Perras* included four members who had decided the earlier appeal.

The first indication of a changing judicial attitude respecting the application of the principle by the Supreme Court came in *Reference re Farm Products Marketing Act*[10] where Rand J. observed that by virtue of the abolition of appeals to the Privy Council, the Supreme Court was not strictly bound by its previous decisions in constitutional cases. Commentators argued that such liberty also extended to non-constitutional cases.[11] However, it was not until the judgment of Cartwright J. in *Binus v. The Queen*[12] that the change was stated in clear and unequivocal terms. In that case, the previous decision under consideration was not overruled but indeed expressly followed and the provincial appellate court rebuked in the name of *stare decisis* for failing to do so. Yet Cartwright J. took the opportunity to open the door to change by stating:

> I do not doubt the power of this Court to depart from a previous judgment of its own but, where the earlier decision has not been made *per incuriam,* and especially in cases in which Parliament or the Legislature is free to alter the law on the point decided, I think that such a departure should be made only for compelling reasons.[13]

---

[7] For example see *Gale v. Bureau* (1911), 44 S.C.R. 305 at p. 315; *Grant v. Scott* (1919), 59 S.C.R. 227.

[8] (1909), 42 S.C.R. 361.

[9] (1908), 41 S.C.R. 244.

[10] [1957] S.C.R. 198 at p. 212.

[11] See Andrew Jones, "Stare Decisis in the Supreme Court of Canada" (1958), 36 C.B. Rev. 175 at pp. 176-7; C.G. Bale, "The Quiet Revolution" (1966), 14 Chitty's L.J. 329 at p. 332; The Honourable E.M. Hall, "Law Reform and the Judiciary's Role" (1972), 10 Osgoode Hall L.J. 399 at p. 403; G.F. Curtis, "Stare Decisis at Common Law in Canada," (1978), 12 U.B.C.L. Rev. 1 at pp. 3-4.

[12] [1967] S.C.R. 594.

[13] *Ibid.* at p. 601.

There is no express indication of what would constitute "compelling reasons," nor is there any indication whether the learned judge had in mind the "very exceptional circumstances" referred to in the Stuart case. It can only be said that Mr. Justice Cartwright did not find such reasons present in *Binus* or in *Peda v. The Queen,*[14] where he repeated his opinion. While both of these were criminal cases there is nothing in either of Mr. Justice Cartwright's statements to indicate that he intended them only in respect of criminal cases.

Dickson J., speaking for the majority in *Barnett v. Harrison,*[15] when invited by counsel to "reappraise" a previous decision, clearly assumed that the court could do so, although he declined to exercise the power in that particular case. He stated:

> Finally, the rule in *Turney v. Zhilka* has been in effect since 1959, and has been applied many times. In the interests of certainty and predictability in the law, the rule should endure unless compelling reasons for change be shown.[16]

Laskin C.J.C., dissenting, with whom Spence J. concurred, was of the opinion that the principle in *Turney v. Zhilka* was not applicable to the case then before the court. Elsewhere the Chief Justice has clearly indicated that in his view the Supreme Court is not strictly bound by the principle of *stare decisis.*[17]

---

[14] [1969] S.C.R. 905 at p. 911 where Cartwright C.J. repreated: "I do not doubt the power of this Court to depart from previous judgments of its own; but I can find no ground sufficient to warrant our refusing to follow the carefully considered judgments of this Court in *O'Grady* and in *Mann* on the point now under consideration . . ." With the exception of Hall and Spence JJ. who concured with Cartwright C.J., the majority were of the opinion that the proposition in the previous cases considered binding by Cartwright C.J. was *obiter* and therefore not binding, and that *Binus* itself was not binding because it was decided with reference to a different section of the Criminal Code.

[15] [1976] 2 S.C.R. 531.

[16] *Ibid.* at p. 559. What was implicit here was made explicit at the 1979 David B. Goodman Lectures, where Mr. Justice Dickson observed extrajudicially: "It is not now doubted that the Supreme Court of Canada can overrule its previous decisions, as and when required." (B. Dickson, "The Role and Function of Judges," The Law Society of Upper Canada Gazette (1980) Vol. XIV, 138 at 184.

[17] See B. Laskin, "The Institutional Character of the Judge" (1972), 7 Israel L.R. 329 wherein the now Chief Justice observed at p. 341 that the principle of *stare decisis* "is no longer an article of faith in the Supreme Court of Canada, but it still remains a cogent principle there;" B. Laskin, "The Role and Functions of Final Appellate Courts: The Supreme Court of Canada" (1975), 53 C.B. Rev. 469 at p. 478; see also a comment in *Vapour Canada Ltd. v. MacDonald* (1976), 7 N.R. 477 at p. 505 contemplating at least a possibility that the court might "retain a cautious concern for *stare decisis*", and see E.M. Hall, "Law Reform and the Judiciary's Role" (1972), 20 Chitty's L.J. 77 at p. 80 where Mr. Justice Hall states: "There is no doubt that the Supreme Court of Canada is not now bound rigidly by [the doctrine of *stare decisis*] and the way is open to depart from previous decisions."

In *Hill v. The Queen*[18] Pigeon J., with whom all of the members of the court concurred on the particular point, overruled the previous decision of the court in *Goldhar v. The Queen*.[19] However, there were two conflicting lines of Supreme Court authority before the court in *Hill* and accordingly Pigeon J., in overruling *Goldhar,* was simply choosing between the two conflicting views which, on any view of the rule of *stare decisis*, the court must do.[20] But in *R. v. Paquette*[21] Martland J., speaking for a unanimous court, declined to distinguish the previous decision of the court in *Dunbar v. The King*[22] on its facts, and expressly overrule it.[23] There is nothing in the judgment which would indicate that the fact that the case was criminal was in any way significant. Indeed, only a few months later, the Supreme Court of Canada speaking through Laskin C.J.C., in a civil case, *McNamara Construction (Western) Ltd. v. The Queen,*[24] overruled the previous decision of the court in *Farwell v. The Queen,*[25] stating simply that the case could "no longer be regarded as an authority. . .".[26] With similar understatement Spence J. in *Bell v. The Queen*[27] stated flatly that the Court was not bound by its previous decision in *Polai v. City of Toronto.*[28]

In *Capital Cities Communications Inc. v. Canadian Radio-Television Commission,*[29] Laskin C.J.C., speaking for the majority of the court, put to rest speculation concerning the binding force of previous decisions of the Privy Council upon the Supreme Court,[30] observing that ". . . this Court is not bound by judgements of the Privy Council any more than by its own judgements." Shortly thereafter in *Reference re Agricultural Products Marketing Act, Farm Products Marketing Agencies*

---

[18] Rehearing before full court: (1975), 62 D.L.R. (3d) 193; originally heard before eight-member court: 23 C.C.C. (2d) 321.

[19] [1960] S.C.R. 431

[20] 62 D.L.R. (3d) 193 at p. 209; see also *Brant Dairy Co. Ltd. v. Milk Commission of Ontario* (1972), 30 D.L.R. (3d) 559 at p. 586-7.

[21] (1976), 30 C.C.C. (2d) 417.

[22] (1936), 67 C.C.C. 20.

[23] *Supra.* f.n. 21, at p. 423.

[24] [1977] 2 S.C.R. 654.

[25] (1894), 22 S.C.R. 553.

[26] *Supra* f.n. 24, at p. 661.

[27] (1979), 98 D.L.R. (3d) 255 at 261.

[28] [1973] S.C.R. 38.

[29] (1978) 18 N.R. 181 at p. 199.

[30] G.F. Curtis, "*Stare Decisis* at Common Law in Canada", (1978), 12 U.B.C.L. Rev. 1, at pp. 4-6.

Act, and The Farm Products Marketing Act,[31] the court confirmed its position by refusing to follow a Privy Council decision, which had however been attenuated in succeeding cases.

Ontario

The Ontario Court of Appeal has been characterized as "the most conservative provincial court"[32] from the standpoint of strict adherence to the doctrine of *stare decisis*. As other courts have proceeded to adopt increasingly liberal attitudes with respect to the binding force of their previous decisions, the characterization may be more dramatic today than it was in 1966 when the statement was made.

In earlier times there was an attempt to reduce the matter to statutory enactment. The Judicature Act of 1895 provided that courts were to be bound by their previous decisions except where the decision was overruled by a higher court or departed from with the concurrence of the judges who gave the earlier

---

[31] [1978] 2 S.C.R. 1198, per Laskin C.J.C. at p. 1257 and per Pigeon J. at p. 1290. The Privy Council decision referred to is *Lower Mainland Dairy Products Sales Adjustment Committee v. Crystal Dairy Ltd.,* [1933] A.C. 168. Not long after, the Court reaffirmed the position in *A.V.G. Management Science Ltd. v. Barwell Developments Ltd.,* [1979] 2 S.C.R. 43, at p. 57, the Chief Justice observing, in respect of *Bain v. Fothergill* (1874), L.R. 7 H.L. 158, that that decision had been applied by the Supreme Court in *Ontario Asphalt Block Co. v. Montreuil* (1916), 52 S.C.R. 541 "at a time when this Court was still subject to the Privy Council and through it to the House of Lords in matters of common law. That situation no longer obtains, and this Court has asserted its freedom not only to depart from its own decisions but from Canadian decisions of the Privy Council as well." The point was anticipated by P.W. Hogg in a Case Comment of *MacDonald v. Vapour Canada Ltd.,* [1977] 2 S.C.R. 134, 54 C.B.R. 361 at p. 370.

[32] Mark MacGuigan, "Precedent and Policy in the Supreme Court" (1967), 45 C.B. Rev. 626 at p. 652.

of Highways,[43] when confronted with a previous decision which he felt unable to distinguish, Middleton J.A. felt compelled to follow the decision notwithstanding that he would have come to the opposite conclusion but for that decision.

In *R. v. Eakins*[44] the Ontario Court of Appeal refused to follow one of its previous decisions because it was of the opinion that to follow it would have involved "overlooking the express terms of the statute." Accordingly, while it is nowhere so stated, it may be that the decision in *R. v. Eakins* is within the *per incuriam* exception to the rule.[45]

Re Gillis[46] appears to be the only instance where the Court of Appeal has expressly refused to follow a previous decision of its own without trying to come within one of the recognized exceptions. In that case Robertson C.J.O. overruled the previous decision in *Re Wright*[47] with the flat statement:

> . . . with every respect to the opinion expressed in *Re Wright*, we are not able to read the provisions of subs. 4 of s. 10 as they were interpreted in that case.[48]

However, the doubt raised by *Re Gillis* as to whether or not the Ontario Court of Appeal considered itself strictly bound by the doctrine of *stare decisis*, was quickly quelled by *Re Hardy Trusts*[49] where Pickup C.J.O. stated that it could not be said that the previous decision being questioned "was given *per incuriam* or was the result of any slip or inadvertence and this Court feels that it is not at liberty to depart from this decision." Similarly, in *Re Smith*,[50] Roach J.A., relying on *Young v. Bristol Aeroplane Co. Ltd.,*[51] stated that the Ontario Court of Appeal "should follow its own earlier decision on a question of law unless it is satisfied that the earlier decision was given *per incuriam*."

In *R. v. DeClercq*[52] MacKay J.A. affirmed the rule in disposing of an issue on the basis that the court was bound by its

---

[43] [1933] O.W.N. 783.

[44] [1943] O.R. 199.

[45] This appears to be the interpretation placed upon it by Professor Friedmann in "Stare Decisis at Common Law and Under the Civil Code of Quebec," 31 C.B.Rev. 723 at p. 729.

[46] [1950] O.W.N. 21.

[47] [1938] O.R. 117.

[48] [1950] O.W.N. 21 at p. 23.

[49] [1955] 5 D.L.R. 10 at p. 11.

[50] [1953] O.W.N. 884 at p. 887.

[51] [1944] K.B. 718.

[52] [1966] 1 O.R. 674 at p. 676.

previous decision in an earlier case. However, Laskin J.A. (as he then was), dissenting, stated quite unequivocally:

> I do not regard this Court as being prevented by any principle of *stare decisis* from reconsidering its previous decisions. [53]

The issue came squarely before the court, in a way in which it had not before, in *Delta Acceptance Corp. Ltd. v. Redman.* [54] This was a hard case in which a decision of the Court of Appeal given three years before had determined a point of statutory interpretation, which was again before the court. McGillivray J.A., who wrote the majority judgment in the earlier case, adopted in *Delta* the literal statutory interpretation propounded in the earlier case, although not entirely without reservation. However, in following the prior decision he found support in the rule of *stare decisis* and in the fact that the plaintiff and a great many others not before the court had relied upon the earlier decision.

Schroeder J.A., who dissented in the previous case, was no more persuaded of the soundness of the majority position when deciding the later case than he had been when deciding the earlier case. But he considered himself bound by the majority judgment in the earlier case and felt compelled to follow it in *Delta.* He stated:

> . . . we are bound by the doctrine of stare decisis to bow to the majority judgment in the [earlier case]. That is a decision of a Court which, though differently constituted, is a Court of coordinate authority and this Court would not be justified in declining to follow it if it should be of opinion that it was wrong. *Stuart v. Bank of Montreal* . . . is authority for the proposition that this Court is bound by its own decisions provided that they enunciate a substantive rule of law . . .
>
> I am impelled to the conclusion that the decision of the majority in the [earlier case] does lay down a substantive rule of law, and although, if unfettered by that judgment, I would decline to give effect to the rule which it must be taken to enunciate, and notwithstanding my strong view that it is inconsistent in its parts, I am bound to give my loyal adherence to the doctrine of *stare decisis* and follow that decision so long as it remains unreversed by a Court of higher authority or the Legislature does not intervene to change it by clarifying the meaning of the section under review by an appropriate amendment. [55]

---

[53] *Ibid.* at p. 677.
[54] [1966] 2. O.R. 37. The prior decision involved here was *Park Motors (Barrie) Ltd. v. Vardy,* [1963] 1 O.R. 57.
[55] *Ibid.* at p. 39.

Laskin J.A. (as he then was), who was not a member of the court which heard the earlier case, delivered a dissenting judgment in *Delta*. He was able to avoid the doctrine of *stare decisis* by drawing a rather convincing distinction between "factual results" and "principles." For this reason Schroeder J.A., in his judgment in *Delta*, undertook a detailed analysis of the earlier decision, concluding that the point in question involved a principle of law and not merely a specific factual determination. Laskin J.A. observed that even where no principle of law is involved, the Court of Appeal "should not lightly depart from a previous decision," and that

> it may be imprudent to refuse to follow an earlier decision (which cannot be distinguished or otherwise explained away) where that decision has either stood for many years on the same bottom of circumstances, or has been reaffirmed by the Court in intermediate cases.[56]

He then concluded that he was justified in his result, since it was the only result which was logically consistent with the principle which emerged from the result in the previous case. The doctrine of *stare decisis* did not, in his view, operate to prevent the reconciliation of result with principle.[57]

In *R. v. Bell*,[58] a situation not unlike that which presented itself to the court in *Delta* again arose. While there was no dissent in the previous case, *City of Toronto v. Polai*,[59] two members of the court which heard *Bell* had also been members of the court which heard *Polai*, one of whom, upon reconsidering the contentious point in the subsequent case, was of the view that the former decision was wrong. MacKinnon J.A., who was not a member of the court which heard the earlier case, stated that that case "was directly on point and that it binds this Court;"[60] however he was also of the opinion that the contentious point should be determined on the merits as it had been in the former case. Jessup J.A., who had concurred with Schroeder J.A. on the particular point in *Polai*, but delivered separate reasons with respect to a different point, concurred in the judgment of MacKinnon J.A. in *Bell*. Brooke J.A. did not specifically deal with the point in *Polai*, but had he disagreed

---

[56] *Ibid.* at p. 51.
[57] *Ibid.* at p. 52.
[58] (1977), 15 O.R. (2d) 425.
[59] [1970] 1 O.R. 483; aff'd [1973] S.C.R. 38.
[60] (1977), 15 O.R. (2d) 425 at p. 428.

with the majority position his result would have had to have been other than it was. In *Bell* he indicated that having had the advantage of argument and the Divisional Court judgment, he had serious doubts that he would have reached the conclusion he did in *Polai*. Nevertheless, he considered the judgment in *Polai* binding and concluded that it was not still open to him to come to a different conclusion.[61] What remains unclear is whether Brooke J.A. considered a departure from *Polai* foreclosed by virtue of the fact that it was a previous decision of the Ontario Court of Appeal, or because the Court of Appeal judgment had been affirmed by the Supreme Court of Canada.[62]

It is interesting to note that in *Re Downtown Oshawa Prop. Owners et al.*,[63] decided a short time before *Bell*, there appears to be an implicit assumption that the question of the binding force of previous Court of Appeal decisions is not necessarily beyond question. In that case Blair J.A. commented:

> It is not necessary to consider whether this Court is entitled to review its previous decision in the *Ontario Steel Products* case, as I am in agreement with the conclusion reached by the majority of that Court [on the merits] . . .

While the Ontario Court of Appeal has only very rarely overruled a previous decision of its own, it has on occasion made very liberal use of techniques permitting circumvention of the rule. For example in *Applebaum v. Gilchrist*[64] a majority of the court overruled a then current line of Ontario authority including two previous decisions of the Court of Appeal on the basis that these previous cases had all relied upon an earlier Court of Appeal decision which the Court as constituted in *Applebaum*, felt could not be considered as a binding authority (a) because the cause of action in the former case was alienation of affection while in the instant case it was loss of consortium, and (b) because in a re-enactment of The Married Women's Property Act which occurred between the original Court of

---

[61] *Ibid.* at p. 426-7.

[62] *Ibid.* at p. 430. The Supreme Court of Canada reversed the decision of the Ontario Court of Appeal (1979), 98 D.L.R. (3d) 255. Spence J., speaking for the majority, did not find it necessary to overrule *Polai* but rather found it to be factually distinguishable. The learned judge declined to pass comment on the issue of the binding effect of its previous decisions on the provincial Court of Appeal, observing at page 261 "I am, therefore, of the opinion that whether or not the Court of Appeal for Ontario were bound by the decision in *Polai* . . . this Court is not bound."

[63] (1976), 13 O.R. (2d) 492 at p. 499.

[64] [1946] 4 D.L.R. 383.

Appeal decision and the subsequent cases, a phrase omitted from one subsection in the 1887 revision of the former Act had been restored to that subsection. The Court of Appeal cases decided subsequent to this re-enactment, having viewed the previous Court of Appeal decision as authoritative and not having made specific reference to the somewhat innocuous alteration in the wording of the statute, were therefore not binding (presumably because they were decided *per incuriam*). Accordingly, the Court was able to come to the admittedly fairer result that it was no longer the law of Ontario that a woman could not maintain a cause of action for loss of matrimonial consortium although a man could. Interestingly, Roach J.A., who dissented in *Applebaum,* did so solely because he felt he must by reason of the doctrine of *stare decisis.* He stated:

> Were it not for the decisions of our own Courts to the contrary, I would most certainly have held the judicial opinion that such a claim as the plaintiff here puts forward constituted a good cause of action at common law. I respectfully bow to those decisions on that point, as I conceive it my duty to do . . . It cannot be said that the judgment in *Lellis v. Lambert* was the result of any inadvertence or slip. The point was squarely before our Court, and I consider the judgment binding upon me.[65]

In *Weatherall v. Weatherall,*[66] as was observed by Wright J. in *Chliwniak v. Chliwniak,*[67] the Court of Appeal effectively overruled its previous decision in *Scott v. Scott,*[68] by distinguishing the case so narrowly that the same court, in the subsequent case of *Beattie v. Beattie,*[69] was able to come to the opposite conclusion on relevant facts identical to those present in the overruled case. In *Scott* a wife's claim for alimony was denied because she had not made written demands for cohabitation and restitution of conjugal rights before commencing the action. In *Weatherall, Scott* was distinguished on the ground that the claim for alimony in *Weatherall* was made by way of counter-claim in the husband's divorce action while *Scott* was an action by the wife for alimony. Moreover, the decision in *Scott* was based upon a requirement under the English divorce rules; but, said the court in *Weatherall,* English law when adopted in

---

[65] *Ibid.* at pp. 410-411.
[66] [1937] O.R. 572.
[67] [1972] 2 O.R. 64 at pp. 72-74; see also "Alimony in Ontario", 7 Fortnightly L.J. 86.
[68] (1930), 64 O.L.R. 422.
[69] [1945] O.R. 129.

Canada does not include English practice. In *Beattie v. Beattie* two members of the Court did not feel compelled to deal with the point in coming to their conclusion and the third simply stated, without specifically referring to *Scott,* that he did not think the proposition established by that case was the law of Ontario.[70]

In *Maskewycz v. Maskewycz,*[71] the Court of Appeal, straining under the restrictions imposed by strict adherence to the rule of *stare decisis* in an area particularly affected by changing social conditions and values, utilized both the device of narrow distinction and that of an expanded *per incuriam* exception in order to reshape the law in keeping with changing values. The Court of Appeal had determined in *Davis v. Davis*[72] that there was a *prima facie* right of a joint tenant to partition or sale, that there was a corresponding obligation on a joint tenant to permit partition or sale, that the court should compel such partition or sale if no sufficient reason appeared why such order should not be made,[73] and that mere inconvenience was not a sufficient reason to refuse the joint tenant's *prima facie* right. Accordingly the wife's application for partition and sale of the premises occupied by the parties as their home and in which the husband and children continued to reside, was granted.

Subsequent cases involving applications for partition by husbands against deserted wives erected a different rule, permitting the wife a right to remain in the matrimonial home. *Bendall v. McWhirter,*[74] which had been relied upon in the Ontario cases, established the wife's right as a quasi-proprietary right in the nature of an irrevocable personal licence. The House of Lords in *National Provincial Bank v. Ainsworth*[75] overruled this aspect of *Bendall v. McWhirter,* finding the wife's right to be purely personal against the husband, basing it either solely upon the duty of each spouse to live with the other, or upon that ground in conjunction with the husband's duty to support his wife.

In *Maskewycz,* in recognition of the increasing equality of rights between husband and wife resulting from changing social conditions, the court held that a deserted husband had rights of occupation with respect to the matrimonial home that were distinct from his right to possession arising from his own joint

[70] *Ibid.* at p. 138.
[71] (1973), 2 O.R. (2d) 713.
[72] [1954] O.R. 23.
[73] *Ibid.* at p. 29.
[74] [1952] 2 Q.B. 466.
[75] [1965] A.C. 1175.

ownership, but that the right should be more readily taken away from him than in the case of a wife, because the wife had a right to support which the husband did not.[76] In so doing it was necessary to confine the previous decision in *Davis* to circumstances not present in *Maskewycz*. The court stated that *Davis* "ought not to be applied to cases where the property in question is the matrimonial home, jointly owned by a husband and wife, where the issue of desertion is raised."[77] Yet the premises which were the subject of the partition application in Davis had "been occupied by [the parties] as their home"[78] and desertion was not mentioned in the judgment solely because, on the court's reasoning in that case, it was irrelevant. Indeed, the notes of argument indicate that if the wife was to be believed, there probably was constructive desertion by the husband by reason of cruelty, and, if not, then there was desertion by the wife. The issue was therefore before the Court in *Davis* and had it been of the opinion that desertion was in any way significant to the proposition propounded, the Court at the very least would have had to address the point.

The second point of interest for present purposes arises from the statement in *Maskewycz* that:

> The overruling of *Bendall v. McWhirter* by the House of Lords in the *National Provincial Bank* case requires this Court to re-examine the decisions in Ontario which were founded upon *Bendall v. McWhirter*. It is not a situation where a line of authority has developed in England, which the courts of Canada may or may not choose to follow (as in *The Queen v. Jennings,* [1966] S.C.R. 532, and *Ares v. Venner,* [1970] S.C.R. 608), but rather a situation in which the courts of Ontario have accepted as persuasive a basis for a right which the House of Lords has since declared was erroneous. We are therefore free to re-examine that right and its basis.[79]

The justification for the invitation to re-examine previous decisions appears to be something of an expanded *per incuriam* exception. Yet the situation is not as it would have been prior to the abolition of appeals to the Privy Council. Presumably the previous Court of Appeal decisions which had considered and adopted *Bendall v. McWhirter* were considered decisions and the law set out therein was the result of original consideration

---

[76] (1973), 2 O.R. (2d) 713 at p. 740.

[77] *Ibid.* at p. 731.

[78] *Davis v. Davis,* [1954] O.R. 23 at p. 27.

[79] (1973), 2 O.R. (2d) 713 at p. 739.

since it cannot be said that the court was in any way bound to follow the English Court of Appeal decision.[80] If the Ontario Court of Appeal is justified in reviewing its previous decisions where the House of Lords has overruled the English Court of Appeal decision upon which former Ontario Court of Appeal decisions were based, then arguably the Ontario Court of Appeal should be justified in reviewing its own decisions when it has not followed other authority but the House of Lords or a judicial body of similarly persuasive stature propounds a different and conflicting principle of law relevant to the same facts. From there it is not a long step to argue that even if no other court has dealt with the problem, it ought to be open to the Court of Appeal to review its previous decision where it concludes the previous decision is wrong.

Just as the logic of the argument for review in *Maskewycz* inclines toward opening the door to unfettered review of previous decisions where the court deems it appropriate, a comment of Martin J.A. in the recent case of *R. v. Gushue*[81] abruptly reaffirms the court's professed strict adherence to *stare decisis*.

---

[80] In *Carnochan v. Carnochan*, [1953] O.R. 887 at pp. 894-5, Schroeder J. (as he then was), quoted a passage from Lord Denning's judgment in *Bendall v. McWhirter*, [1954] 2 Q.B. 466 at p. 477, to the effect that the deserted wife's right to stay in the matrimonial home proceeds out of an irrevocable authority which the husband is presumed in law to have conferred on her which flows from the status of the marriage coupled with the fact of separation owing to the husband's misconduct, and which authority remains until the court orders her out. He then observed: "It would seem, therefore, that the right of a deserted wife to stay in the matrimonial home proceeds out of an irrevocable personal licence which the husband is presumed in law to have conferred on her. In *Bendall v. McWhirter* her occupation is said to be comparable with that of a contractual licensee save that her licence is not revocable except by an order of the Court." In exercising his discretion under s. 12 of The Married Women's Property Act Schroeder J. permitted the wife to continue in occupation of the matrimonial home. In upholding the trial judge's decision Laidlaw J.A., speaking for the Court of Appeal ([1954] O.W.N. 543 at p. 544), stated: "We are unable to perceive any error in principle in the exercise of the discretion vested in the learned judge under s. 12 of The Married Women's Property Act."

In *Re Jollow v. Jollow*, [1954] O.R. 895 at p. 902-3, after quoting another passage from Lord Denning's judgment in *Bendall v. McWhirter (supra* at pp. 476-7) to the effect that the wife's right arises out of the irrebuttable presumption of law that she has irrevocable authority to pledge the husband's credit for necessaries, Chevrier J.A. continued: "That decision of course is not binding in this Province, but in my opinion the logic of Denning L.J. is so compelling that it should be followed."

In *Rush v. Rush* (1960), 24 D.L.R. (2d) 248 at p. 252, after quoting the same passage from *Bendall v. McWhirter* as was quoted in *Re Jollow v. Jollow*, and after referring to domestic authority on the point, Schroeder J.A. stated: "The principle which I deduce from the English and Ontario authorities is that the right of a deserted wife to stay in the matrimonial home proceeds out of an irrevocable licence which the husband is presumed in law to have conferred upon her."

[81] (1976), 14 O.R. (2d) 620.

There it was observed that should inconsistency arise between a previous Ontario Court of Appeal decision and a House of Lords decision, the court would be bound by its former decision.[82]

The dilemma of observing the dictates of *stare decisis* at the expense of justice between the parties again presented itself to the court in *Fenn v. City of Peterborough.*[83] The case is significant because of the directness of the court's reasoning in refusing to follow its previous decision.

The case involved a claim by the plaintiffs in connection with a natural gas explosion which demolished their house, personally injured one of the plaintiffs, and killed their three children. In early August, one of the defendants, the Peterborough Utilities Commission, excavated around a gas main while replacing a water service line. As a result of improperly backfilling the excavation, stress was placed upon the gas main which fractured in early January, permitting gas to escape into the plaintiffs' house which resulted in the explosion.

The defendant utility raised in its defence the six month limitation period provided under the Public Utilities Act.[84] The action was instituted in early July, less than six months after the explosion. The defendant contended that the limitation period commenced to run from the date of the improper backfilling as oppposed to the date that the plaintiffs sustained damage. This interpretation was manifestly inequitable since the plaintiffs' action might well become proscribed before the cause of action had accrued.

In advancing its defence of proscription the defendant utility relied upon the decision of the Ontario Court of Appeal in *Davies v. Traders Finance.*[85] In that case the plaintiff had purchased a truck at a sheriff's auction. Unknown to him, but known to the sheriff, the vehicle was subject to the defendant Traders' security interest under a conditional sales contract registered in another county. Nine months later, Traders seized the vehicle from the plaintiff and sold it. The plaintiff instituted action just less than six months after the seizure, claiming against the sheriff for breach of warranty. The sheriff relied upon the six month limitation period under the Public

---

[82] *Ibid.* at p. 629. It was stated in *R. v. Demeter* (1976), 10 O.R. (2d) 321 at p. 343 that tne Ontario Court of Appeal was not bound by the House of Lords in *The Sussex Peerage* (1844), 11 Cl. & Fin. 85.

[83] (1979), 25 O.R. (2d) 399. The reasons were delivered "By the Court" constituted by five members.

[84] R.S.O. 1970 c. 390, s. 32.

[85] (1959), 18 D.L.R. (2d) 48.

Authorities Protection Act,[86] successfully arguing that time commenced to run at the time of the sale by the sheriff to the plaintiff, notwithstanding that the plaintiff could not have known of the breach until the seizure by the defendant, nine months later.

Despite acknowledged similarity betweeen the two statutory provisions, the court in *Fenn* declined to follow the earlier decision in *Davies*. While the court did not expressly overrule *Davies,* in refusing to follow it, it observed that it was doing so on reasoning "which is more direct" than that of the trial judge below but which, "having regard to what was said in *Davies v. Traders Finance Corp. Ltd.,* . . . may not have appeared to the judge to have been open to him."[87]

The phrase which the Court in *Fenn* was required to construe read as follows:

> No action shall be brought . . . but within six months next *after the act* committed.[88]

The phrase construed in *Davies* was:

> No action . . . shall lie . . . unless it is commenced six months next *after the act.* . .[89]

In delivering its reasons the court in *Fenn* twice acknowledged the similarlity in language between the two provisions,[90] but held against the construction in *Davies,* that the phrase "the act committed" in s.32 of The Public Utilities Act must be construed as meaning "the cause of action arose."[91] In doing so the court observed that the statutory language in question

> is capable of the more restrictive interpretation which would confine "act" solely to the conduct of the defendant, isolated from its legally significant consequences. This approach was apparently adopted in *Davies*. . .[92]

There is nothing in the language of the decision in *Fenn* from which it may be fairly concluded that the court was expressly

---

[86] R.S.O. 1950 c. 303, s. 11.

[87] *Supra,* f.n. 83 at 415.

[88] *Supra,* f.n. 84 s. 32.

[89] *Supra,* f.n. 86 s. 11.

[90] *Supra,* f.n. 83 at pp. 416, 421.

[91] *Ibid.* at p. 417.

[92] *Ibid.* at p. 418.

overruling its previous decision in *Davies*. Nor can it be said that under the doctrine of *stare decisis* strictly applied, the court in *Fenn* was necessarily bound by its previous decision in *Davies;* this is so because notwithstanding the acknowledged similarlity of statutory language, the court in each case was construing a different statute. Yet from an analytical perspective the two decisions cannot stand together, and if the point in observing strict application of the doctrine is to be more than a matter of form, one would not expect that the same statutory language could be construed differently solely because different statutes were concerned.

Certainty in the law was not an issue since the relevant section of The Public Authorities Protection Act construed in *Davies* had been amended by the time of *Fenn* to obviate the inequitable result established in *Davies;* yet while certainty may be the rationale of the doctrine, its absence does not constitute a recognized exception to *stare decisis*. While it may conceivably provide some explanation for the unreservedness of the court's refusal to follow *Davies,* it is more remarkable that in doing so the Court did not appear to be at pains to distinguish the previous case. It was observed that the principle in *Davies* did not properly lie to be applied because on the facts of that case the cause of action had technically accrued at the time of the act complained of;[93] but that result would be no less inequitable, and had the court in *Fenn* intended that this was a basis for avoiding the *Davies* decision, one would expect a concluding observation that the decision was therefore made *per incuriam*.

Just as the decision in *Fenn* seems to signal a softening in the strictness of the Court's application of *stare decisis*, its decision only seven months later in *A. G. for Ontario v. Palmer*[94] confirms its continued adherence to the principle in all its rigour. It would appear that the decision in *Fenn* was simply an instance of the court clearing away the authoritative force of a previous decision no longer in tune with accepted values, in circumstances where it could do so without departing from its professed philosophy of strict adherence to *stare decisis*. In the *Palmer* case the court could not do so, and at least one member felt compelled to defer to the authority of the earlier line of decisions when he would not otherwise have done so. That judge, significantly, was Blair J.A., who, some three and one-half years before, appeared to

---

[93] *Ibid.* at p. 422.
[94] (1979), 28 O.R. (2d) 35.

entertain some doubt as to the binding force of the court's previous decision.[95] In *Palmer* he observed:

> With reluctance I concur with the conclusion reached by my brother Zuber. If I had not considered myself bound by the authorities, to which he has referred, I would have adopted the judgment of Southey, J.[96]

A distinction has been established in Ontario between civil and criminal cases in the application of the doctrine of *stare decisis.* English origins of the distinction can be found as early as 1877 in the observations of Lord Chancellor Cairns in *Ridsdale v. Clifton.*[97]

> In the case of decisions of final Courts of Appeal on questions of law affecting civil rights, especially rights of property, there are strong reasons for holding the decisions, as a general rule, to be final as to third parties.
>
> The law as to rights of property in this country is to a great extent based upon and formed by such decisions. When once arrived at, these decisions become elements in the composition of the law, and the dealings of mankind are based upon a reliance on such decisions. . .
>
> On the other hand, there are not, in cases of this description, any rights to the possession of property which can be supposed to have arisen by the course of previous decisions; and in proceedings which may come to assume a penal form, a tribunal, even of last resort, ought to be slow to exclude any fresh light which may be brought to bear upon the subject . . . .
>
> These considerations have led their Lordships to the conclusion that, although very great weight ought to be given to the decision in *Hebbert v. Purchas,* yet they ought in the present case to hold themselves at liberty to examine the reasons upon which that decision was arrived at, and if they should find themselves forced to dissent from those reasons, to decide upon their own view of the law.

Similarly, Lord Halsbury stated in *Read v. Lincoln:*[98]

> . . . their Lordships cannot but adopt the view expressed in *Ridsdale v. Clifton* as to the effect of previous decisions. Whilst fully sensible of the weight to be attached to such decisions, their Lordships are at the same time bound to examine the reasons upon which the decision rests, and to give effect to their own view of the law.

---

[95] *Supra,* f.n 64.
[96] *Supra,* f.n. 94.
[97] (1877), 2 P.D. 276 at pp. 306-7.
[98] [1892] A.C. 644 at p. 655.

The special rule applicable to criminal cases achieved full statement in *R. v. Taylor*[99] where the full court unanimously overruled its prior decision in *R. v. Treanor.*[100] Lord Goddard, speaking for the court, observed:

> The Court of Appeal in civil matters usually considers itself bound by its own decisions . . . In civil matters this is essential in order to preserve the rule of stare decisis . . . [The Court of Criminal Appeal], however, has to deal with questions involving the liberty of the subject, and if it finds, on reconsideration, that, in the opinion of a full court assembled for that purpose, the law has been either misapplied or misunderstood in a decision which it has previously given, and that, on the strength of that decision, an accused person has been sentenced and imprisoned it is the bounden duty of the court to reconsider the earlier decision with a view to seeing whether that person had been properly convicted. The exceptions which apply in civil cases ought not to be the only ones applied in such a case as the present . . .

The distinction between criminal and civil matters was recognized as early as 1920 by the Appellate Division of the Alberta Supreme Court in *R. v. Hartfeil*;[101] however, except for a passing comment by McRuer C.J.H.C. in *R. v. Northern Electric Co. Ltd.*[102] that "the rule may be more flexible in criminal cases than it is in civil cases," the matter does not appear to have been applied in Ontario prior to the decision of Jessup J.A. in *R. v. Thornton.*[103] There, relying upon *R. v. Taylor,* the majority refused to follow the court's previous decision in *R. v. Yaskowitch*[104] Interestingly, in *R. v. Nelson*[105] the decision in *Thornton* was itself effectively overruled and *Yaskowitch* reaffirmed. Also in *R. v. Olbey*[106] the court overruled its earlier decisions in *R. v. Sutton*[107] and *R. v. Spatola*[108] (although not expressly) to the detriment of the liberty of the subject.

---

[99] [1950] 2 K.B. 368 at p. 371. See also *R. v. Gould*, [1968] 2 Q.B. 65 at p. 68; *R. v. Newsome*, [1970] 2 Q.B. 711 at p. 716; *D.P.P. v. Merriman*, [1972] 3 W.L.R. 545 at p. 563.

[100] [1939] 1 All E.R. 330.

[101] [1920] 3 W.W.R. 1051 per Stuart J. at p. 1056 and Beck J. at p. 1062.

[102] [1955] O.R. 431 at p. 445.

[103] [1971] 1 O.R. 691, 2 C.C.C. (2d) 225.

[104] [1938] O.R. 178; 70 C.C.C. 15.

[105] [1972] 3 O.R. 174; 8 C.C.C. (2d) 29.

[106] [1971] 3 O.R. 225; 4 C.C.C. (2d) 103.

[107] [1970] 2 O.R. 358, [1970] 3 C.C.C. 152.

[108] [1970] 3 O.R. 74; [1970] 4 C.C.C. 241.

It was not until the decision of Martin J.A. in *R. v. McInnis*[109] that the exception in *R. v. Taylor* became established beyond question in Ontario; the court stated that "in criminal cases where the liberty of the subject is involved, the Court is not bound by its previous decisions to the same extent as in civil matters." However "in matters of ciminal law *stare decisis* is to be strictly adhered to unless a benefit to the liberty of the subject is involved. It is of the utmost social importance that there be certainty in the criminal law."[110]

British Columbia

In contrast with the Ontario Court of Appeal, the British Columbia Court of Appeal has, from the earliest times, taken a far more flexible approach to the doctrine of *stare decisis*. As early as 1912, a majority of the British Columbia Court of Appeal declined to follow an earlier decision of its predecessor, the "full court," on the basis that while the rule of judicial comity is a salutory one, "it must yield in some cases to considerations which are paramount to it in importance." Such considerations were seen to be present in *Re Rahim*[111] where adherence to the former decision in *Ikezoya v. C.P.R.*[112] would have established "[a] practice in conflict with the practice in England, and would prejudicially affect the liberty of the subject." Similarly, in *McDonald v. B.C. Electric Ry. Co.*[113] Martin J.A. refused to follow a decision of the predecessor full court, commenting that

> while as a rule I think we should follow the decisions of that Court (and invariably do in regard to practice, procedure and juridical matters on our Provincial statutes, in order to avoid confusion and uncertainty in the working of this Court), yet cases may arise where the circumstances are so exceptional as to require our independent consideration . . .

[109] (1973), 1 O.R. (2d) 1 at p. 11. See also *R. v. Li*, (unreported, Ontario Court of Appeal, released Nov. 4, 1975) per Jessup J.A.; *R. v. Santeramo* (1976), 32 C.C.C. (2d) 35 at p. 46.
[110] *R. v. Govedarov, Popovic & Askov* (1974), 3 O.R. (2d) 23; aff'd 25 C.C.C. (2d) 161. See also *R. v. Maika* (1974), 27 C.R.N.S. 115 at p. 116; *Ex Parte Pickett* (1976), 12 O.R. (2d) 195 at p. 200.
[111] (1912), 17 B.C.R. 276 at p. 279. This was a 3:1 decision, Irving J.A. dissenting on the ground that the former decision should be followed (at p. 281).
[112] (1907), 12 B.C.R. 454. Without it being expressly so stated, this decision was also overruled in *Re Tiderington*, (1912), 17 B.C.R. 81, as noted by MacDonald C.J.A. in *R. v. Gartshore* (1919), 27 B.C.R. 175 at p. 179.
[113] (1911), 16 B.C.R. 386 at p. 400.

In *Gentile v. B.C. Electric Ry. Co.*[114] the court again addressed itself to the question of overruling previous cases, and though the court spoke with the caution befitting a general statement, the principle was stated in terms somewhat broader than the traditional *per incuriam* exception. MacDonald C.J.A. expressly allowed that a previous decision of the Court of Appeal as well as its predecessor, the Full court, might be overruled "if we were convinced beyond all question that that decision was wrong; that it had gone upon a wrong principle, or contrary to some well-established authority which had not been brought to the attention of the Court."[115] Martin J.A. referred to his statement in *McDonald v. B.C. Electric Ry. Co., supra,* and Galliher J.A. stated:

> If, speaking for myself, it appears clear to me that the decision of the Full Court is palpably wrong, that is, if it is based on absolutely wrong conclusions, or a misconception probably of some authorities decided by some other Court, then I think that it is not the duty of this Court to perpetuate the error, if that error is manifest; and I think we have good English authority for that proposition. A start has to be made some time in setting right what has been decided wrongly, and somebody is apt to suffer. It should not be lightly made, and it should only be made where a Court is absolutely satified that the judgement relied on is erroneous, and not merely a case where they might come to a different conclusion.[116]

Again in *R. v. Gartshore*[117] a majority of the court allowed that in certain circumstances it might review its own decision and accordingly permitted counsel to argue that a previous decision ought to be overuled. Interestingly, a minority of two, of whom Martin J.A. was one, would not have permitted counsel to argue the point, insisting that there must be finality to the rulings of the court.[118] Yet in *Ex p. Yuen Yick Jun*[119] Martin C.J.B.C., who had dissented in *Re R. v. McAdam,*[120] expressly refused to follow that case, relying on *Re Rahim, supra,* and stated that the "decision in *McAdam's* case should in my opinion

---

[114] (1913), 18 B.C.R. 307.
[115] *Ibid.* at p. 309.
[116] *Ibid.* at p. 310.
[117] (1919), 27 B.C.R. 175.
[118] The majority was composed of MacDonald C.J.A. at p. 179, Galliher J.A. at pp. 182-3, and Eberts J.A. at p. 183; the minority was composed of Martin J.A. at pp. 180-182 and McPhillips J.A. at p. 183.
[119] [1940] 2 D.L.R. 432.
[120] [1925] 4 D.L.R. 33.

'yield . . . to considerations which are paramount to it in importance' ".[121]

In *Bell v. Klein (No. 1)*[122] the British Columbia Court of Appeal again considered its ability to review a previous decision. Sloan J.A., dissenting, although not denying the propriety of so doing, was of the opinion that the court's previous decision in *Staples v. Issaacs (No. 2)*[123] was correctly decided.[124] Robertson J.A., with whom O'Halloran and Bird JJ.A. concurred, was clearly of the opinion that the court could overrule its previous decision, but appeared to confine the power to the *per incuriam* exception. He stated:

> Where material cases or statutory provisions are not brought to the attention of a court and the court is satisfied that the decision was given *per incuriam*, it is not bound to follow its previous decision.[125]

However it was a non-binding Ontario Court of Appeal decision not referred to the court in *Stapes v. Isaacs, supra,* which the learned judge relied upon to justify overruling the prior case. Sidney Smith J.A., with perhaps greater candor, simply stated:

> Much argument was directed here as to whether the *stare decisis* principle allowed us to overrule a former decision; but we have done it before, and personally I think we not only can do it again, but should do so if we are satisfied that the former decision was wrong.[126]

Rather than stretching the *per incuriam* exception, he simply disagreed with the previous decision:

> It seems to me, respectfully, that the whole substance of the court's decision in *Staples v. Isaacs,* as tersely put in the leading judgement, . . . is that 'where there is no protection there can be no compulsion'. For my part, and with great deference, I find myself quite unable to agree with this proposition, for which I can see no legal warrant.[127]

In *R. v. Haas*[128] the British Columbia Court of Appeal sitting as a five-member court, unanimously overruled the court's

---

[121] *Supra* f.n. 119 at p. 435; see also O'Halloran J.A. at p. 442.
[122] (1954), 12 W.W.R. (N.S.) 272.
[123] [1940] 2 W.W.R. 657.
[124] *Supra,* f.n. 122 at p. 274.
[125] *Ibid.* at p. 280.
[126] *Ibid.* at p. 289.
[127] *Ibid.* at p. 290.
[128] (1962), 35 D.L.R. (2d) 172.

previous decision in *R. v. White*[129] under circumstances in which doing so was to the detriment of the liberty of the subject. The various members of the court simply stated that they adopted or preferred the dissenting reasons of Martin J.A. over those of the majority in the prior case.

In *Forsythe v. Forsythe*[130] a majority of the British Columbia Court of Appeal refused to follow a previous decision of long standing on the basis that that decision had inferentially been overruled by the Supreme Court of Canada. Davey J.A., who dissented, referred to *Young v. Bristol Aeroplane Co. Ltd.*[131] as establishing that the English Court of Appeal considers itself bound by its previous decisions, with certain limited exceptions, and continued:

> But this Court has assumed the power to overrule through a division of five Judges its previous decisions, if convinced that they were wrongly decided . . .

However, he cautioned:

> The power which we have assumed to overrule our previous decisions is an encroachment on the principle of *stare decisis,* and ought to be most carefully exercised . . .[132]

Alberta

In the first half of this century the Appellate Division of the Supreme Court of Alberta seemed to be of the view that it was not strictly bound by its previous decisions. However, its present position appears to be somewhat unsettled.

As early as 1910 the Alberta Supreme Court *en banc* in *Re Ryley Hotel Co. Ltd.*[133] declined to follow its previous decision in *Re Richelieu Hotel Licence,*[134] on the basis that under the circumstances the court was effectively the final court of appeal and the "Court should decline to follow its own earlier decision — at least when so recent — if on further consideration it is of

---

[129] [1926] 3 D.L.R. 1.
[130] (1965), 56 D.L.R. (2d) 322.
[131] [1944] 2 All E.R. 293.
[132] *Supra.* f.n. 130 at p. 325.
[133] (1910), 15 W.L.R. 229.
[134] (1909), 10 W.L.R. 402.

opinion that the former decision was wrong".[135] Ten years later, Beck J., in declining to follow a previous decision, expressed his view of the matter in much stronger terms. He stated in *Reventlow-Criminil v. R.M. of Streamstown:*[136]

> I have little respect for the maxim *stare decisis*, and, on the contrary, think that unless in exceptional cases the sooner a Court rejects a decision, whether of its own or of another Court whose decision is not that of a Court which has jurisdiction on appeal from itself, the better.

Again in *R. v. Hartfeil,*[137] in refusing to follow the court's previous decision in *R. v. Schmolke,*[138] Beck J. reiterated:

> I feel bound not to refrain from expressing my real opinion upon questions of substantial importance notwithstanding a decision of this division to the contrary.[139]

Stuart J., who had dissented in *R. v. Schmolke, supra,* declined to follow the majority in *Hartfeil,* observing that the scope of the principle of *stare decisis*

> has been practically confined to civil cases . . . And the general principle seems to rest mainly upon the desirability of giving certainty to the property and contractual rights of parties who may have, upon advice of their solicitors, acted upon the faith of a decision.[140]

Accordingly, in view of the facts that it was a criminal matter before the court, a five-member bench had assembled, no property or contract rights were involved, the previous decision was very recent and was not a considered opinion given on the merits but rather was the simple adoption of a decision from another province in the interests of comity, convenience and desirable uniformity, Stuart J. felt the court was at liberty to question it.

Ives J., who declined to follow the previous decision, did not expressly address the issue. Harvey C.J.A., dissenting, felt that the previous decision should be followed, observing that, with

---

[135] *Supra* f.n. 133 per Beck J. at p. 236 (with whom Scott J. concurred, Stuart J. dissenting). Interestingly, the Supreme Court of Canada granted leave to appeal and unanimously reversed the judgement (43 S.C.R. 646) notwithstanding that it had refused leave to appeal in the overruled case on the basis that the trial judge was *persona designata*.

[136] [1920] 1 W.W.R 577 at p. 586.

[137] *Supra,* f.n. 101.

[138] [1919] 3 W.W.R. 409.

[139] *Supra,* f.n. 101 at p. 1062.

[140] *Ibid.* at p. 1056.

one exception, it had been the court's "uniform practice since it was established to consider itself bound by its previous decisions"[141] and that "unless this Court intends to establish a new principle of decision for itself it must follow its previous decisions unless, of course, it is shown that some decision or some provision of law has been overlooked . . . ."[142]

In *Dowsett v. Edmunds*[143] Harvey C.J.A., speaking for a five-member court, including Beck J.A., stated that a previous decision of the court "was binding on the learned trial judge below as it is on us and unless and until it is overruled by a higher court it declares the law of this province on the point in question."

Similarly, in *R. v. Selock*[144] McGillivray J.A., dissenting from the majority judgement of Harvey C.J.A., felt bound by the previous decisions of the court which the Chief Justice felt able to disregard by reason of an intervening amendment to the Criminal Code. In *Chekaluck v. Sallenback,*[145] counsel had argued that a decision of the Supreme Court of Canada had inferentially overruled previous Alberta decisions notwithstanding that a previous decision of the Appellate Division given subsequent to the Supreme Court of Canada decision had held that the previous Alberta decisions were unaffected. Harvey C.J.A. replied to the argument: "Even if this were so, it would not justify this Division in refusing to follow its previous decision."

In decisions of more recent vintage, the court appears more to have assumed than decided that it is bound by its previous decisions. The knowledge that other western appellate courts have renounced a restricted position may well be the reason why the court has avoided authoritive affirmation of its position; or again it may be that the court has been fortunate in not having been squarely faced with the issue in recent years. In *R. v. Mankow*[146] the Appellate Division affirmed the decision of a district court judge on trial *de novo,* reversing the decision of a magistrate who in dismissing an information expressed the view that he was not bound by an earlier decision of the Appellate Division because it had been inferentially overruled by the Supreme Court of Canada. The majority of the Appellate

---

[141] *Ibid.* at p. 1052.
[142] *Ibid.* at p. 1054.
[143] (1926), 22 Alta. L.R. 292 at p. 303.
[144] [1931] 2 W.W.R. 745 at pp. 761 and 765.
[145] [1948] 1 W.W.R 510 at p. 512.
[146] (1959), 22 D.L.R. (2d) 667.

Division in *R. v. Mankow* did not share the learned magistrate's view that the earlier decision had been overruled, and Boyd McBride J.A., in *obiter dicta,* affirmed that the court was bound by its previous decisions. He stated:

> By the rule as to *stare decisis,* subject to well understood exceptions having no application here, a judgement of this Division is binding on it and also on the trial Judges of this Court and on all lower Courts within the Province. Furthermore, unless and until it is declared wrongly decided or overruled or modified by the Supreme Court of Canada or by appropriate legislation, it declares the law of this Province on the point . . . [T]he belief that a higher Court would take a different view from that expressed by this Division, though founded on general reasoning in other cases decided by the higher Court, is not a sufficient reason for not following the decision of this Division.[147]

The position propounded by Boyd McBride J.A. is extreme in that it appears to view the court as bound by its previous decision even under circumstances in which the previous decision is inconsistent with a decision of the Supreme Court of Canada, so long as that court has not expressly overruled or modified the previous decision. It cannot be said that the other members of the court necessarily shared this view. The Chief Justice was simply of the opinion that the previous decision had not been overruled and that it was binding, at least on the district court judge. Johnson J.A., dissenting, pointed out that the determinative test applied by the Appellate Division in the previous decision was incorrect and that the correct test was that set out by the Supreme Court of Canada in a subsequent case. He then observed:

> My concept of *stare decisis* does not compel me to perpetuate a test for determining the validity of legislation which is at variance with one which has been settled by superior Courts which we are bound to follow.[148]

In *Texas Gulf Sulphur Co. v. Ballem,*[149] in refusing to follow a statement made by the court in a previous case on the ground that it was *obiter,* Cairns J.A. referred to the decision of the Supreme Court of Canada in *Stuart v. Bank of Montreal*[150] and remarked:

---

[147] *Ibid.* at p. 672.
[148] *Ibid.* at p. 677.
[149] (1970), 17 D.L.R. (3d) 572.
[150] (1909), 41 S.C.R. 516.

The observations on the doctrine of *stare decisis* of Anglin, J. (as he then was), are also very clear and definite on the importance of Courts following their own decisions. This decision has of course been followed on many other occasions [by the Supreme Court of Canada] . . . and, of course, it has been followed by our Courts on many occasions.

Unfortunately the learned judge does not cite any Alberta cases. Again in *Brook and Sunnybrook Holdings Ltd. v. Calgary,*[151] Clement J.A. commented:

It is a principle of law, expressed in the term stare decisis, that like cases should be decided alike; and I assume for the purposes of this decision that the principle applies to judgements of this Court, without examining the submission to the contrary made by counsel for the appellants, since it is not neccessary to do so in view of the conclusion I have reached.

It was not necessary for the learned judge to settle the issue one way or the other, since, as was the case in *Texas Gulf v. Ballem,* he found the statement in the previous decision relied upon to be *obiter dicta* and not binding.

Saskatchewan

During the first half of this century the Saskatchewan Court of Appeal seemed inclined to the view that it was not necessarily bound by its previous decisions. However, the court has not dealt with the issue in recent years; consequently, if its liberal attitude of earlier times has changed, there does not appear to be any contemporary statement to indicate the change.

In *Wolfe v. Canadian National Railways*[152] the court refused to follow its previous decision in *Mills v. Sherwood Stores Ltd. (No. 2).*[153] Turgeon J.A., who delivered the judgment of the court, stated:

In dealing with the case of *Mills v. Sherwood Stores Ltd.,* I am aware of the difficulty which confronts a Court when it is asked to refuse to follow one of its own previous decisions . . . But here the situation is peculiar. The decision in question seems to stand by itself and to be inconsistent with other decisions of the Court delivered both before and after it, and in which the Court proceeded on the interpretation of the statute which I have adopted in this case . . . In view of this situation, I think it

---

[151] [1971] 1 W.W.R. 429 at p. 433; aff'd [1971] 5 W.W.R. 96 (S.C.C.)
[152] [1934] 3 W.W.R. 497.
[153] [1918] 2 W.W.R 1030.

advisable, for the guidance of those whose duty it is to administer this statute, to declare that the rule laid down by the majority judgment in *Mills v. Sherwood Stores Ltd.*, should not be followed.[154]

A somewhat more striking example of the Saskatchewan Court of Appeal refusing to follow a previous decision which it considered to be wrongly decided is found in *Davidson v. Davidson.*[155] There Martin C.J.S., speaking for a five-member court, determined that the previous decision in *Pettit v. Pettit*[156] was wrongly decided. The court had held in that case that an affidavit denying collusion and connivance in a divorce action was necessary under s. 41 of the English Divorce and Matrimonial Causes Act 1857, incorporated into the law of Saskatchewan by The North-West Territories Act[157] and that there was no jurisdiction in the court to relieve against the failure to supply such; however in *Davidson* the court was of the opinion that s. 41 "is procedural and is not substantive law" and

[f]ailure on the part of this court to recognize the contents of sec. 41 as procedural was the cause of the decision in *Pettit v. Pettit.*[158]

On the basis of this, the Court simply stated that "[t]he decision in *Pettit v. Pettit* . . . should, therefore, be disregarded."[159] The example is striking because it was a clear overruling in circumstances not coming within the exceptions to the rule of *stare decisis* outlined in *Young v. Bristol Aeroplane,*[160] unless the *per incuriam* exception includes misinterpretation of a statutory enactment. Of course, if this is the case, it widens the exception considerably.

---

[154] *Supra*, f.n. 152 at p. 506. The point involved concerned the interpretation to be placed upon what was then s. 15 of The Workmen's Compensation Act, R.S.S. 1930, c. 262. The other decisions referred to by Turgeon J.A. which he maintained were inconsistent with the court's decision in *Mills v. Sherwood Stores Ltd.*, were *Kier v. Bennell* (1914), 7 W.W.R. 15 and *Hewitson v. Robin Hood Mills, Ltd.*, [1924] 1 W.W.R. 143, both of which were distinguishable from the case at bar on the basis that both dealt with injured workmen and propounded a measure of damages applicable only to an injured workman who continued to live, while *Mills* and the case at bar were both concerned with compensation for the dependants of a deceased workman, *Mills* establishing that under the Saskatchewan Act there was no distinction between partial and entire dependancy in assessing compensation.

[155] (1952), 7 W.W.R. 272; see also G.D. Kennedy, "Case and Comment," (1953), 31 C.B.Rev. 87.

[156] [1938] 2 W.W.R. 253, also a decision of Martin J.A., as he then was.

[157] 49 Vict., c. 25.

[158] *Supra* f.n. 155 at p. 275.

[159] *Ibid.* at p. 277.

[160] [1944] 2 All E.R. 293.

Manitoba

The Manitoba Court of Appeal, like its Saskatchewan counterpart, has unequivocally established that it is not necessarily bound by its previous decisions. The earliest case illustrating the point is a somewhat stark example. In *Bullock v. Hansen*[161] the court declined to follow its previous decision in *Contant v. Pigott*[162] without so much as oral reasons. Then in *R. v. Thompson*,[163] in the face of severe criticism of its previous decision in *Demchenko v. Fricke*[164] by the appellate courts of other provinces, the court declined to follow that decision, Fullerton J.A. observing:

> My first impression was that we were bound by our earlier decision but I find that other Courts, when convinced of the error of their previous decisions, have refused to follow them . . . Convinced as I am that the construction placed upon the section of the statute in question here by this Court in *Cole v. Friesen* . . . is erroneous and that the construction placed upon it by the Saskatchewan Court of Appeal is the correct one, I think it is our right, as well as our duty, to say so and to give effect in the case at bar to what we now believe to be the correct interpretation of the section.[165]

Dennistoun J.A. commented:

> The doctrine of *stare decisis* does not compel a court to perpetuate error. I have frequently said that the Court of Appeal of the provinces should endeavour to reconcile their views whenever possible for obvious reasons, and when satisfied of error to frankly acknowledge it.[166]

There was a momentary weakening of the position in *Benson v. Harrison*[167] where Adamson J.A., in a dissenting judgment, relied upon a previous decision of the court which the majority distinguished, and, citing *Stuart v. Bank of Montreal*, commented that "[t]his court should not depart from a decision of its own." However, the view did not gain favour. In *Daudrich v. Daudrich*[168] the court declined to follow a comment of

---

[161] (1928), 37 Man. R. 450.
[162] (1913), 5 W.W.R. 946.
[163] [1931] 1 W.W.R. 26.
[164] [1926] 2 W.W.R. 221.
[165] *Supra*, f.n. 163 at p. 28.
[166] *Ibid.* at p. 31.
[167] (1951), 4 W.W.R. 225 at p. 231.
[168] (1971), 22 D.L.R. (3d) 611.

Monnin J.A. in *Whyte v. Whyte*[169] (which, however, appears to have been *obiter*), and in *R. v. Radford*[170] the court declared that its previous decision in *Campbell v. Sumida*[171] "should no longer be regarded as authoritative," after observing that the decision had been explained and qualified in subsequent decisions and "constantly criticized and not followed" by courts in other provinces.[172]

If there was any doubt as to the court's position, it was placed beyond question in *General Brake & Clutch Service Ltd. v. W.A. Scott & Sons Ltd.*[173] wherein the court's previous decision in *Kare v. North West Packers Ltd. and McGuckin et al.*[174] was overruled. Freedman C.J.M. stated:

> Let me at once express my belief that we do not lack the power to depart from an earlier decision of this Court. It is a power that will of course be exercised only in rare circumstances. But if the circumstances are deemed appropriate and we are convinced that the earlier decision was incorrect we should be guided by the principle that it is no part of the function of any Court to make error perpetual.[175]

Quebec

Quebec, a civil law jurisdiction, has never been as concerned with the doctrine of precedent as have the common-law provinces.

In the days when the Supreme Court of Canada considered itself strictly bound by the doctrine of *stare decisis,* it refused to make any differentiation between appeals from common law and civil law courts.[176] Quebec courts themselves, unlike their

---

[169] (1969), 7 D.L.R. (3d) 7.

[170] (1973), 13 C.C.C. (2d) 575.

[171] [1965] 3 C.C.C. 29.

[172] *Supra,* f.n. 170 at p. 576.

[173] (1975), 59 D.L.R. (3d) 741.

[174] [1955] 2 D.L.R. 407.

[175] *Supra* f.n. 173 at p. 742.

[176] In *Groulx v. Bricault* (1921), 63 S.C.R. 32 at p. 43, Mignault J. stated "D'ailleurs la décision rendue dans *Meloch v. Simpson* nous lie, et la question se trouve ainsi résolue définitivement." In somewhat stronger language Anglin C.J.C. stated in *Daoust, Lalonde & Cie Ltée v. Ferland,* [1932] S.C.R. 343 at p. 351: "Nor will it do to say that, although *stare decisis* may be a good enough doctrine for the rest of Canada, it forms no part of Quebec jurisprudence and it, therefore, should not be applied in this court to cases from that province. Here, the old idea, *ubi jus est aut vagum aut incertum, ibi maxima servitus praevalebit,* still obtains. In my opinion, the doctrine of *stare decisis* must equally apply in the determination of any case which comes before this court whatever may be the province of its origin." See also *Village of Malbaie v. Boulianne,* [1932] S.C.R. 374.

counterparts in France,[177] generally recognize the applicability of the doctrine as between higher and lower courts.[178] While the former Court of Queen's Bench (Appeal Side) (and presumably equally its successor, the Quebec Court of Appeal) recognized the principle of *stare decisis,* the court has never considered itself strictly bound by its previous decisions. This is evidenced as early as 1893 by the overruling in *Reid v. McFarlane*[179] of two previous decisions on the basis that they had been grounded upon an erroneous interpretation of an earlier Privy Council decision.

Similarly, in *Migner v. St. Lawrence Fire Insurance Co.*[180] the court departed from two previous decisions on the ground that they wrongly interpreted the law and that the relevant French literature had been overlooked. In *Lavasseur v. Pineau,*[181] Langlais J., exercising trial jurisdiction of the Superior Court, refused to follow the 1889 Supreme Court of Canada decision in *Shaw v. Cadwell*[182] which he considered to be wrong. This rather striking example appears to be supported by the observations of Bissonnette J. in the Queen's Bench appeal decision in *Bellefleur v. Lavallée.*[183] The learned trial judge stated:

> Si important que puisse paraître avoir l'autorité d'un précédent, celle-ci n'est pas telle, toutefois, qu'elle constitue une règle jurisprudentielle définitive, d'autant moins qu'en principe la Cour d'appel de cette province n'est pas liée par les arrêts de la Cour suprême du Canada. Et cette liberté d'action se justifie davantage quand, selon l'opinion qui prévant dans le Québec, le motif juridique du jugement est erroné . . .

---

[177] The *Cour de Cassation* only binds a lower court in the particular case under review but has no direct authority with respect to future cases. See Plaiol, *Traité Elementaire de Droit Civil,* 5th ed., (1950) at s. 128.

[178] Greenshields C.J. reprimanded the trial judge in *O'Kane v. Dame Palmer* (1938), 78 Q.S.C. 296 at p. 299 for an apparent disregard of higher court decisions in the following terms: "I make reference to the judgements that have been rendered in this matter for the sole purpose of remarking that I accept them in their entirety, and to further remark, that the learned trial judge, with whose judgment I am now dealing, has apparently, steadfastly neglected or refused to follow the rule known as 'Stare decisis', which, being translated, means, 'Abide by authorities or cases already adjudicated upon.' " Similarly Archambault J. admonished in *Mazurette v. Cité de Montréal,* [1942] C.S. 210 at p. 211: ". . . bien que les tribunaux de la province de Québec ne reconnaissent pas la doctrine *stare decisi,* il est dans l'intérêt de l'administration de la justice que les juges de la Cour supérieure ne rendent pas de décision contraire aux arrêts de la Cour du banc du roi; . . . ."

[179] (1893), Q.R. 2 Q.B. 130.

[180] (1900), 10 Que. K.B. 122.

[181] [1951] S.C. 448.

[182] (1889), 17 S.C.R. 357.

[183] [1957] R.L. 193, at pp. 204-205. See also Castel, *The Civil Law System of the Province of Quebec* (1962) at p. 229.

En conclusion, il faut donc dire avec Rivard que "les précédents n'ont, dans notre système judiciaire, qu'une autorité de raison: leur valeur ne peut venir que de leurs motifs. Les raisons qui ont inspiré la décision d'un tribunal l'emportent sur le fait que cette décision a été rendue; quand un point déjà jugé se présente de nouveau, la Cour d'appel peut donc considérer les décisions antérieures et en tenir compte, mais moins pour tabler sur le fait même de ces précédentes que pour en découvrir les motifs, les apprécier au regard de la loi, des principes et de la logique."

New Brunswick

On two occasions in the last century the New Brunswick Supreme Court, exercising an appellate jurisdiction, displayed a flexible approach to the doctrine of precedent, by overruling its previous decisions.[184] In recent times the Appeal Division appears to have adopted a more conservative attitude. While Limerick J.A. has stressed the need for judicial creativity in

---

[184] In *R. v. Commissioners of Germantown Lake District* (1869), 12 N.B. R. 341, Ritchie C.J., speaking for the majority, in refusing to follow a previous decision of the court, observed at pp. 356-7: "In shewing cause, not without some reason, great stress was laid on the fact that there had been already an adjudication on the very point in controversy, and that until reversed by an Appellate Court that decision was binding. It is no doubt generally most convenient and desirable to adhere strictly to the decisions of the Court once pronounced, leaving further discussion and reversal, if found wrong, to a higher tribunal, and this observation would be entitled to more weight if such Appellate Court was practically accessible to the great body of suitors in this Province. But we can discover no arbitrary and inflexible rule requiring this in all cases. If there were two conflicting decisions we should be bound to elect, or if any previous authority more in our opinion in accordance with the law had been accidentally overlooked, or if the decision ignores, or is in our opinion inconsistent with, the right application of a clear and well-established and important principle we think the case should give way to the principle, and this is no novel view, for we find constantly throughout the books cases explained, questioned, doubted, disapproved and overruled or not acted on, by others than Courts of Appellate Jurisdiction, and therefore, though we think a decision once deliberately declared should not be lightly disregarded or disturbed unless by Court of Appeal, except for cogent reason and upon a clear manifestation of error, there are occasions when we should be wrong to shut our ears or refuse our judgment, and this, we think, is one of those exceptioned cases." Similarly in *Black v. Brown* (1894), 32 N.B. Rep. 631 the Supreme Court of New Brunswick sitting as a five member court overruled its previous decision in *Sullivan v. Murphy* (1888). 27 N.B.R. 172.

order that law develop to meet the needs of a changing society, [185] on two more recent occasions he has held that the court is strictly bound by its previous decisions. In *Re Ramsey*, [186] Limerick J.A. was faced with the very peculiar circumstance of a provincial court judge granting a request of the Crown that two remaining trials arising out of the same facts be heard by another judge in order to avoid possible bias arising out of the judge's findings in a prior trial in which the judge ordered an acquittal because he disbelieved the crown witnesses. In granting prohibition against any other judge hearing the remaining two trials, he stated:

> When this Court or any other court makes a finding based on specific circumstances the decision should be considered as a precedent establishing the finding that court would make in any future case on identical circumstances. An informant or plaintiff, if that decision be unfavourable to him, would know it would be pointless to commence similar proceedings unless he is prepared to carry the proceedings to a higher court by way of an appeal. [187]

In *Ford Motor Credit Co. v. Sorensen*[188] Limerick J.A., while expressly preferring the dissenting reasons of McNair C.J.N.B. in the court's previous decision in *Taylor v. Traders Finance Co.*, [189] held that he was bound by the majority judgment in that case "unless set aside by a decision of the Supreme Court of Canada." He continued:

> If this court were to find otherwise, this court differently constituted could at some future date again reverse this finding leaving an

---

[185] *Subsurface Surveys Ltd. v. John Burrows Ltd.* (1967), 62 D.L.R. (2d) 700, where he observed at pp. 723-4: "Reasons sound in themselves under conditions existing some 20 years ago are not necessarily applicable today; competition, lessening of moral standards, pressures brought about by the decreasing amount of profit one can retain because of higher taxation all lead to sharper and more unethical business practices. It is the duty of the Court to see that the law expands with the growth and development of the country, and changing conditions should lead to co-extensive changes in the application of the law. If the Courts continue to follow decisions made 20, 50 or 100 years ago without reference to changing conditions, moral standards, economic and social developments, justice will be ill-served . . .

"One of the duties of the Court is to see that justice as well as law is administered. The enforcement of law by the Court not tempered with justice will gradually create a disregard for the Courts as well as for the law and result in the undermining and final destruction of our judicial system, the safeguard against injustice, oppression, bureaucracy and autocracy in our constitutional system."

[186] (1972), 4 N.B.R. (2d) 809.

[187] *Ibid.* at pp. 813-14. While the language employed seems directed to the principle of *stare decisis*, the issue is probably more aptly characterized as coming within the broad principle of *res judicata*.

[188] (1973), 6 N.B.R. (2d) 40.

[189] (1959), 43 M.P.R. 139.

impossible situation in that the law would change at the whim of the court sitting at the time.[190]

Nova Scotia

There appears to have been very little judicial consideration of the issue in Nova Scotia, with the possible exception of *R. v. Walsh*[191] in which a four member court overruled the court's previous decision in *R. v. McDonald;*[192] however, the court did so on the basis that the decision was inconsistent with an earlier decision of the Privy Council in *Colonial Bank of Australia v. Willan.*[193]

Prince Edward Island

In *Ford v. MacLeod*[194]the Prince Edward Island Supreme Court *in banco* overruled its previous decision in *Acorn v. MacDonald,*[195] although in so doing it relied upon an intervening conflicting decision of the Supreme Court of Canada, and upon new provincial legislation. In *Gunston v. Montreal Trust Co.*[196] the Prince Edward Island Court of Appeal in Equity, apparently overruled the earlier unreported judgment of the Supreme Court *in banco* in *Royal Exchange Assurance v. Montreal Trust Co.*[197]

The position was recently affirmed in *R. v. Ostridge,*[198] a decision of a single judge of the Prince Edward Island Supreme Court[199] in appeal from a decision of a Provincial Court judge. There M.J. McQuaid, J. assumed that the Court *in banco* exercising civil jurisdiction could vary its prior decision and went on to recognize the established exception in criminal cases where the liberty of the subject is involved.[200]

The position is somewhat anomalous. The criminal law

---

[190] *Supra,* f.n. 188 at p. 48.

[191] (1897), 29 N.S.R. 521.

[192] (1886), 19 N.S.R. 336.

[193] (1874), L.R. 5 P.C. 417. The recent decision of the Appeal Division in *R. v. MacPherson* (1980), 36 N.S.R. (2d) 674, although not concerned directly with the principle of *stare decisis*, evidences a liberal attitude of the court toward judicial creativity.

[194] [1955] 2 D.L.R. 46.

[195] [1929] 3 D.L.R. 173.

[196] See M. MacGuigan, "Precedent and Policy in the Supreme Court," (1967), 45 C.B.Rev. 649, n. 181 at p. 654, cited as (1955), unreported, no. 1123.

[197] *Ibid.* at p. 654, f.n. 182 cited as (1948), unreported, no. 5601.

[198] (1979), 22 Nfld. & P.E.I.R. 123, 129-130.

[199] Except under particular statutory provisions as here, the court normally exercises appellate jurisdiction by three members sitting *in banco.*

[200] See *supra* pp. 40 et seq.

exception developed precisely as such, viz., an exception to the general rule of strict application. However, as conceived by McQuaid, J. the true exception is that *stare decisis* will be strictly applied only where it operates to the benefit of the liberty of the accused. One wonders why the reliance interests of the accused cannot be entrusted to the protection of the court without resort to an inflexible exception which, by reason of its absolute nature, more often than not may benefit the accused wholly in the absence of reliance.

Newfoundland

In *Re Doyle*[201] the Chief Justice of Newfoundland, though not specifically dealing with the binding force of previous decisions, made some interesting observations respecting that court's approach to technical objections, which may be indicative of how the court would approach the doctrine of *stare decisis*.

Furlong C.J.N. stated:

> I believe that where persons approach this Court with real or imagined grievances they should be heard as fully and as freely as possible and that strict adherence to matters of form and procedure are now treated less gravely than they used to be in earlier days. My own view on these matters can best be expressed, I think, by quoting what is said by the learned author of *Judicial Review of Administrative Action*, S.A. de Smith on page 502 '. . . but the trend has been to place a higher value on the interest of justice than on conformity with established precedents.'[202]

Some twenty-two years earlier, Dunfield J., delivering the majority judgment of the Supreme Court of Newfoundland (on appeal) in *Power v. Winter,*[203] epitomized the liberal approach to the issue of *stare decisis*, although he was not in that case concerned with a previous conflicting decision of his own court. He stated:

> "We are not here to administer the law according to precedent; we are here to do practical justice, guided in essentials by precedent. The two attitudes are quite different. If precedent hinders practical justice, precedent should be stretched. If a court of equal status with ourselves has once or even twice, altered as we all do at times, a generality which is rather wide, must we all follow that generality? I think not."[204]

[201] (1976), 6 Nfld. & P.E.I.R. 479 at p. 483.
[202] *Ibid.* at p. 483.
[203] (1952), 30 M.P.R. 131.
[204] *Ibid.* at p. 148.

Chapter 4

Stare Decisis in Australian and New Zealand Appellate Courts

Australia

The Australian court system is similar to that in Canada: Canada and Australia share the same legal heritage. For these reasons it is extremely useful to examine the Australian courts' attitudes towards the doctrine of *stare decisis*.

As will be seen, Australian courts have often considered the extent to which they are bound by their own decisions. However, it would appear that the most controversial issue in the area of precedent in Australia has been the role of English precedents in Australian decisions. The leading High Court of Australia decisions in this regard are *Waghorn v. Waghorn,*[1] *Piro v. W. Foster & Co. Ltd.,*[2] *Wright v. Wright,*[3] *Parker v. The Queen*[4] and *Skelton v. Collins.*[5] The controversy has also touched the state supreme courts.[6] The position now seems to be that

---

[1] (1942), 65 C.L.R. 289.

[2] (1943), 68 C.L.R. 313.

[3] (1948), 77 C.L.R. 202.

[4] (1962-63), 111 C.L.R. 610.

[5] (1965-66), 115 C.L.R. 94, especially Kitto J. at p. 104 and Owen J. (with whom Windeyer J. concurred) at pp. 137-8. See also a pamphlet by the present Chief Justice, The Rt. Hon. Sir Garfield Barwick, "Precedent in the Southern Hemisphere," 1970. One commentator has boldly suggested that some of the cases in which the High Court criticised House of Lords "precedents" was a contributing factor leading to the 1966 *Practice Statement:* See E. St. John, "Lords Break from Precedent: An Australian View" (1967), 16 Int. Comp. L.Q. 808. And see *Atlas Tiles Ltd. v. Briers* (1978), 52 Aust. L.J.R. 707 (H.C.); *State Government Insurance Commission (S.A.) v. Trigwell* (1979), 53 Aust. L.J.R. 656 (H.C.); and J.K. Bentil, "Authority of English Appellate Courts' Jurisprudence before Australian Supreme Courts" (1977), 5 U. Tas. L. Rev. 307. For a discussion of the same question in the context of the Hong Kong courts, see *de Lasala v. de Lasala*, [1979] 2 All E.R. 1146 (J.C.P.C.).

[6] See, for example, *Scott v. Willmore & Randell*, [1949] V.L.R. 113 (Vict. Sup. Ct.), *R. v. Bugg*, [1978] V.R. 251 (Vict. Sup. Ct. F.C.)

Australian courts are not technically bound by high English authorites; however, they often follow them in preference to previous contrary decisions of their own. While the issue of the binding effect of English decisions is beyond the scope of this study, it is certainly worth noting in general terms as an indicator of the extreme deference Australian courts have shown to English decisions. Indeed, it may well be regarded as merely another facet of the particular aspect of *stare decisis* upon which this study focuses, because it is clear that the general trend in Australia is that appellate courts do not regard themselves as absolutely bound by their own decisions.

Pattern of Appeals

Briefly, the structure of appellate courts in Australia is as follows: Most State Supreme Courts contain no separate "court of appeal," but rather form into "full courts" (usually three-judge panels) to hear appeals from trial decisions of single Supreme Court judges, or in County Court matters. Since 1965, there has existed in New South Wales alone a Court of Appeal Division of the Supreme Court. The High Court of Australia hears appeals from the various State full courts. The panels in the High Court normally consist of three or more.[7]

High Court judges seem to regard the High Court as the final appellate court in Australia for practical purposes. The right of appeal to the Judicial Committee of the Privy Council has been severely curtailed.[8] Appeals to the Privy Council have been abolished except for matters within s.74 of the Australian Constitution[9] in which the High Court has seen fit to grant a certificate. However, s.3(1) of the Privy Council (Limitation of Appeals) Act, 1968 provides that:

> Special leave of appeal to Her Majesty in Council from a decision of the High Court may be asked only in a matter in which the decision of the High Court was a decision that:

---

[7] The High Court Procedure Act 1903-1973 defines a "full court" of the High Court as "two or more Justices of the High Court sitting together."

[8] For a recent discussion of the Privy Council appeal situation see Edward St. John, "The High Court and the Privy Council; The New Epoch" (1976), 50 Aust. L.J. 389. And see "The High Court and the Privy Council", (1978) 52 Aust. L.J. 345; "The High Court and No Privy Council?", (1979) 53 Aust. L.J. 59; "The Authority of Privy Council Decisions in Australian Courts" (1978), 9 Fed. L.R. 427; *Viro v. The Queen* (1978), 18 A.L.R. 257 (H.C.); and *National Employers' Mutual General Association Ltd. v. Waind and Hill (No. 2)*, [1978] 1 N.S.W.L.R. 466 (N.S.W.C.A.).

[9] 63 & 64 Vict. c.12.

(a) was given on appeal from a decision of the Supreme Court of a State given otherwise than in the exercise of federal jurisdiction; and

(b) did not involve the application or interpretation of —
    (i) the Constitution;
    (ii) a law made by the Parliament; or
    (iii) an instrument (including an ordinance, rule, regulation or by-law) made under a law made by the Parliament.

In a nutshell, the only possible appeals to the Privy Council will involve questions regarding the limits *inter se* of the powers of the Commonwealth and the States, or of a state vis-à-vis another state, if the High Court certifies it (an unlikely occurrence, according to some commentators). However, there still exists a direct right of appeal to the Privy Council from State Supreme Courts.

Against this backdrop will be examined various statements made by the High Court of Australia and the State Supreme Courts with respect to the binding effect of their own decisions.

High Court of Australia

The paragraphs below will examine, first, the general statements made by the High Court and, second, several constitutional decisions of the High Court in which the *stare decisis* doctrine has been discussed. The constitutional area in Australia, as in Canada, seems to be a fertile source of pronouncements on the binding effect of precedent and thus will serve as a useful case study.

One of the earliest statements of policy is contained in *Australian Agricultural Company et al. v. Federated Engine-Drivers and Firemen's Association of Australasia*[10] in which Isaacs J.,[11] after an interesting and exhaustive discussion of the practice of appellate courts in other jurisdictions in that era, concluded that the High Court is not bound by its own prior decisions, and that if in the Court's opinion a prior decision is manifestly wrong it is the duty of the Court to overrule that decision. Isaacs J. appeared to be influenced by the fact that the Privy Council, by whose decisions the High Court was bound, had clearly adopted that approach to *stare decisis*.

---

[10] (1913), 17 C.L.R. 261. See also *The Tramways Case (No. 1)* (1914), 18 C.L.R. 54.
[11] (1913), 17 C.L.R. 261 at p. 274 ff.

In *Perpetual Executors and Trustees Association of Australia Limited v. Federal Commissioner of Taxation*[12] Latham C.J.[13] stated:

> Continuity and coherence in the law demand that, particularly in this Court, which is the highest court of appeal in Australia, the principle of *stare decisis* should be applied, save in very exceptional cases.
>
> The Court is not bound by its previous decisions so as absolutely to preclude reconsideration of a principle approved and applied in a prior case, but . . . the exceptions to the rule are exceptions which should be allowed only with great caution and in clear cases.

The well-known case of *Mutual Life & Citizens' Assurance Co. Ltd. v. Evatt*[14] contained some useful observations on *stare decisis*. Barwick C.J.[15] noted that the High Court can freely express the law on a subject as appropriate to current times in Australia. In his view the House of Lords in 1966 reached the position of the High Court of Australia, i.e. "free to overrule its own decision in order properly to express the common law." For Barwick C.J. the *Practice Statement*

> is a useful indication of the balance which needs to be sought between the maintenance of a stable system of law and the provision of rules which are appropriate to do and to ensure justice in current situations. It recognises rightly . . . that the perpetuation of error by an ultimate court of appeal is not an indispensable nor a desirable feature of a stable system of law grounded on judicial precedent.

As Dixon C.J. rhetorically asked in *Commissioner for Railways (N.S.W.) v. Cardy,*[16] after commenting on the fictitious glosses that had grown around unpopular precedents, "why should we here continue to explain the liability which that law appears to impose in terms which can no longer command an intellectual assent and refuse to refer it directly to basal principle?"

In the recent case of *Geelong Harbor Trust Commissioners v. Gibbs Bright & Co.*[17] the High Court again endorsed the

---

[12] (1949), 77 C.L.R. 493.

[13] *Ibid.* at p. 496.

[14] (1968), 122 C.L.R. 556.

[15] *Ibid.* at pp. 563, 564.

[16] (1959-60), 104 C.L.R. 274 at p. 285.

[17] (1970), 122 C.L.R. 504. And see L.V. Prott, "When Will a Superior Court Overrule Its Own Decision?" (1978), 52 Aust. L.J. 304; and R.C. Springall, "Stare Decisis As applied by the High Court to its Previous Decisions" (1978) 9 Fed. L.R. 483.

principles of the House of Lords' *Practice Statement*. Barwick
C.J.[18] observed that the High Court is:

> not bound by any authoritative construction of the words of the section
> it is called upon to construe. It is quite free so far as precedent is
> concerned to place its own construction upon the section . . . The Court
> in my opinion within limits of the kind mentioned by the Lord
> Chancellor in his announcement to which I have referred, should be
> ready to depart from the reasoning of an earlier case where it is
> convinced that that reasoning is clearly wrong and that the rights of the
> citizens should not for the future be tied to conclusions founded upon it.

McTiernan and Menzies JJ.[19] asserted that a court of appeal
should not be too closely fettered by what has been decided
earlier.

In *Geelong Harbor,* however, the majority in the High Court
actually followed an earlier decision which had stood for fifty
years because it was felt that commerce in Australia had been
based upon it. The Privy Council refused to interfere in what was
essentially a matter of local legal policy. It confirmed that the
High Court of Australia has always had the power to refuse to
follow its own decisions, a power which, however, "has been used
but sparingly.[20] . . . The decision whether or not to exercise it is,
in their Lordships' view, one of legal policy into which wider
considerations enter than mere questions of substantive law. The
fact that the court considers its previous decision to have been
plainly wrong is a prerequisite to discarding it, but is by no
means a decisive reason for doing so."[21]

As was mentioned above, numerous constitutional cases
contain statements of the High Court's views on *stare decisis.*[22]
Hughes and Vale Proprietary Limited v. N.S.W. (No.1)[23]
involved one narrow aspect of state regulation of inter-state
trade and commerce. Dixon C.J.[24] was prepared to follow a
previous decision of the High Court, notwithstanding that it
"could not be reconciled with principle" and the grounds upon
which it had been decided for the most part had been rejected by

---

[18] *Ibid.* at pp. 509, 516.
[19] *Ibid.* at p. 518.
[20] [1974] A.C. 810.
[21] *Ibid.* at p. 818.
[22] For a discussion of *stare decisis* in the context of American constitutional law, see J.N. Noland, "*Stare Decisis* and the Overruling of Constitutional Decisions in the Warren Years" (1969), 4 Val. U.L.R. 101.
[23] (1952-53), 87 C.L.R. 49.
[24] *Ibid.* at p. 69 ff.

the Privy Council, because it was a recent decision which had been fully considered and nothing had occurred since to alter the circumstances. He apparently would have been prepared to overrule the previous decision if its impact on the broad area of trade and commerce had been greater than it actually was. (Dixon C.J. may well have foreseen that the Privy Council would later reverse the decision, as in fact happened.)[25] McTiernan J.[26] adopted this approach:

> The principle of *stare decisis* cannot be eliminated from constitutional cases without danger to the stability of law, for important economic and social legislation rests upon the decisions of this Court. The *Transport Cases* confirm the Transport Acts of all the States. These cases could not be reversed without danger to the good order and government of the States, or without casting doubts upon the validity of Commonwealth Acts regulating inter-State commerce and communications, and State Acts besides the Transport Acts. The principle of *stare decisis*, of course, is not rigid and decisions upon the Constitution are not irreversible by this Court. If such decisions were not open to review by the Court the Constitution might become obsolete as an instrument of government. Fresh interpretations of grants of legislative power and of constitutional guarantees may be needed to adapt them to new or changed conditions. It is also right for the Court to depart from a decision which is manifestly wrong, whether it involves the interpretation of a grant of power or a guarantee against certain exertions of power.

Kitto J.[27] agreed that it was "undesirable that a question decided by the Court after full consideration should be re-opened without grave reason."

In *Victoria v. Commonwealth*[28] members of the Court differed over whether a previous decision as to the constitutionality of a provision in a taxing statute should be followed. Dixon C.J. and Kitto J. took the "exceptional course" of declining to follow the decision because (i) it was an isolated decision, receiving no support from prior decisions and forming no part of a line of authority, (ii) it gave an application to the constitutional doctrine of incidental powers which could have great consequences and which was thought to be unsound; and

---

[25] [1955] A.C. 241.

[26] *Supra*, f.n. 23 at p. 76.

[27] *Ibid.* at p. 102.

[28] (1956), 99 C.L.R. 575.

(iii) the question fell within s.74 of the Constitution and affected the States in other ways aside from the immediate taxing issue. Williams and Fullagar JJ. preferred to follow the prior decision because virtually all States were parties to that early litigation and the legislation had subsisted since then without challenge from any State, and the present challenge was sustained by only two States.

In a case in the area of inter-state commerce, *Damjanovic & Sons Pty. Limited v. Commonwealth*,[29] Barwick C.J.[30] stated that he "would not wish to be taken as suggesting that settled constitutional doctrine emerging from the decisions themselves and the ultimate conclusions on which they are based, should not generally be maintained, and only overturned or departed from when its error is clearly made out." Windeyer J.[31] felt that the Court was not

> governed by words, formulae and sentences culled here and there from judgments in other cases on different facts. That does not mean that we are to ignore authoritative expositions in earlier cases, or disregard the facts of earlier cases, as illustrations of the operation of the section in the Constitution. These cases establish doctrine, expound principle and, by denotation, give a concrete content to the abstract and general words of the enactment. This restrains the predilections and idiosyncrasies of an individual judge from dominating his interpretation of the Constitution. It thus makes for a stable law and a stable economy. Speaking in a general sense, I therefore hold myself guided, if not strictly governed, by the earlier decisions of this Court on this topic.

Significantly, Windeyer J. was also of the view that reasoning by analogy is a different process in the development of the common law from its use in the interpretation and application of a statute or of the Constitution.

The comments of Jacobs J. in the very recent case of *H.C. Sleigh Ltd. v. State of South Australia*[32] are noteworthy:

> The principle of *stare decisis* has a particularly important application in a field such as the limits of the taxing powers of the States. The difficult and delicate balance between the Commonwealth and the States on fiscal matters may be currently being preserved upon the basis of decisions previously given by this court. A previous decision of this

---

[29] (1967-68), 117 C.L.R. 390.
[30] *Ibid.* at p. 396.
[31] *Ibid.* at pp. 407-408.
[32] (1977), 12 A.L.R. 449 at pp. 471-2.

court should not be overruled unless the court is convinced not only that it was wrongly decided but that adherence to the decision is leading to social, economic or political consequences which cannot be tolerated by the nation, consequences perhaps not foreseen when the decision was given. The fact that the consequences of decisions in constitutional cases cannot be readily altered by the legislature must result in a willingness, when necessary, to review a previous decision but on the other hand there must be a reluctance so to do unless circumstances compel such a review.

It would appear that the High Court of Australia is perhaps more reluctant to reconsider its previous decisions in the constitutional area. It has done so, however, on a sufficient number of occasions to generate some recent criticism.[33]

State Supreme Courts

The following cases are illustrative of the attitudes of various State Supreme Courts. The decisions of the New South Wales courts have been stressed in particular.[34]

It has always been clear that the Supreme Court of New South Wales has power to overrule its own decisions.[35] In *Bridges v. Bridges and Hooper*[36] Jordan C.J.[37] said:

> I recognise that a considered judgment of the Full Court should not be lightly disregarded; but there is no principle in force in New South Wales which constrains us, as the Court of Appeal has recently held itself to be constrained in England [in *Young v. Bristol Aeroplane Co., Ltd.*] to follow an earlier decision if we are satisfied that it is wrong; and I do not think that we should tie our hands by the introduction of such a principle.

In *Keough v. Heffernan*[38] Jacobs J. placed some qualifications on the rule, thus:

[33] See, for example, Sir Arnold Bennett, "The High Court of Australia — Wrong Turnings" (1977), 51 A.L.J. 5; but see, by the same author, "The Territories Representation Case — *Stare Decisis* in Constitutional Cases" (1978), 52 Aust. L.J. 664, dealing with the significant recent case of *Queensland v. The Commonwealth* (1977), 52 Aust. L.J.R. 100 in which *stare decisis* prevailed over a majority of the Justices' own views of the constitutionality of a statute. And see comments in (1978), 52 Aust. L.J. 302 and 304; and (1978), 9 Fed. L.R. 375.

[34] See a useful treatment of this topic in C.J.F. Kidd, "*Stare Decisis* in Intermediate Appellate Courts: Practice in the English Court of Appeal, the Australian State Full Courts, and the New Zealand Court of Appeal" (1978), 52 Aust. L.J. 274.

[35] *Edwards v. Hirschman* (1900), 21 L.R. (N.S.W.) 116 (N.S.W. Sup. Ct. F.C.).

[36] (1944), 45 N.S.W.S.R. 164 (N.S.W. Sup. Ct. F.C.).

[37] *Ibid.* at p. 172.

[38] (1961), S.R. (N.S.W.) 535 (N.S.W. Sup. Ct. F.C.).

Although this Court . . . is not bound by its previous decisions, nevertheless I do not consider that it is free to differ from a line of decision where one decision is of long standing and the second of them has recently applied and approved the earlier decision. I think this is particularly so where the question is one which concerns the interpretation of a statute . . . .

Richardson v. Mayer[39] contains a very useful review of New South Wales cases touching on the question of *stare decisis*. It also refers to what appears to be a novel procedural innovation — the right of counsel to argue that a previous decision of the Court is wrong should be subject to obtaining leave of the Court to do so. However, this was questioned in *Bennett & Wood Ltd. v. Orange City Council*[40] where it was said that "an absolute rule that leave must be obtained in all cases before an earlier decision can be assailed is too rigid. It is not always observed in the courts which state it as a rule of practice." In this case, Walsh J.A.,[41] while acknowledging that "this rule of practice [i.e., *stare decisis*] has never been regarded as inflexible," nevertheless warned of the danger of confusion if precedents were overlooked. Wallace P.,[42] however, adopted a more liberal approach:

The cases where this Court will not follow such earlier decisions will of course be rare . . . But such cases, rare though they will be, should not I think be confined intransigently to decisions which are "manifestly" or "demonstrably" wrong . . . Giving full credit to the desirability of certainty in the law (which occasionally appears to be a rather pious aspiration) I consider that even an intermediate Court of Appeal may, on special occasions and in the absence of higher authority on the subject in hand, play its part in the development of the law and in ensuring that it keeps pace with modern conditions and modern thought and, accordingly, in an appropriate case I do not think an earlier decision of the Court (including this Court) should be allowed to stand where justice seems to require otherwise.

Finally, in *Flanagan v. H.C. Buckman & Son Pty. Ltd. et al.,*[43] Hutley A.J.A.[44] stated that while the Court of Appeal clearly can

---

[39] [1964-5] N.S.W.R. 105 (N.S.W. Sup. Ct. F.C.).

[40] [1967] 1 N.S.W.R. 502 (N.S.W. Sup. Ct. C.A.) at p. 512.

[41] *Ibid.* at p. 505.

[42] *Ibid.* at pp. 503-4.

[43] [1972] 2 N.S.W.L.R. 761 (N.S.W. Sup. Ct. C.A.).

[44] *Ibid.* at p. 781. See also *Connor v. Sankey,* [1976] 2 N.S.W.L.R. 570 and *De Romanis v. Sibraa,* [1977] 2 N.S.W.L.R. 264; and a comment in (1978) 6 Aust. Bus. L.R. 93.

reconsider its own decisions, the correct rule is that it can only do so when it appears that the prior decision was manifestly wrong. In this case, even if the precedent had been "manifestly wrong" Hutley A.J.A. would have been prepared to follow it, for it had stood for twelve years and had been acted on in much litigation.

In South Australia, the Full Court is free to reconsider a previous decision if, but only if, it is satisfied that its previous decision is clearly wrong.[45] In *Jenerce Pty. Ltd. et al. v. Pope*[46] Mitchell and Wells JJ. in the Full Court, curiously, seemed to inject a *Young v. Bristol Aeroplane Co.* test, but ultimately fell into line with some of the New South Wales cases discussed above.

Generally speaking, it is well established in the other States that appellate courts are not strictly bound by their own prior decisions.[47] Cases from the other Australian jurisdictions will be considered in other contexts in later portions of this study.

New Zealand

The position of the New Zealand Court of Appeal is, for practical purposes, merely an extension of the Australian experience. It is clear that for many years the superior appellate tribunal in New Zealand has been able to overrule its earlier decisions.

Virtually everything that can be said on this question is contained in the very exhaustive discussion in *Re Rayner*.[48] There it was confirmed that the New Zealand Court of Appeal is free to overrule a judgment of that Court which is contrary to the current of New Zealand authority theretofore existing. It was said in that case that the operation of the *Young* doctrine is limited to the practice in England. In New Zealand, because of the prohibitive cost of appeals to the Privy Council, the Court of Appeal is for all practical purposes the final appellate tribunal.

Apparently the accepted practice is for both Divisions of the New Zealand Court of Appeal (the Full Court of Appeal) to sit together to reconsider a prior decision of that Court; in fact, this

---

[45] *Raynal v. Samuels* (1974), 9 S.A.S.R. 264 (S.A. Sup. Ct. F.C.) *per curiam* at p. 273; *R. v. White*, [1967] S.A.S.R. 184 (S.A. Sup. Ct. F.C.) reversed on other grounds, 42 A.L.J.R. 10 (H.C.); *R. v. Barnes* (1978), 20 S.A.S.R. 1 (S.A. Sup. Ct. F.C.).

[46] [1971] 1 S.A.S.R. 204 (S.A. Sup. Ct. F.C.).

[47] The only suggestion to the contrary is found in an old West Australia case, *Transport Trading & Agency Co. of West Australia Ltd. v. Smith* (1906), 8 W.A.L.R. 33 (W.A. Sup. Ct. F.C.) in which Parker C.J. had some doubts at pp. 35-36.

[48] [1948] N.Z.L.R. 455.

was done in *Re Rayner.* Fair J.[49] subjected *Young v. Bristol Aeroplane Co., Ltd.* to rather severe criticism and concluded, "it seems that there should be a means of correcting a decision which is obviously erroneous, even at the possible risk of such power involving uncertainty in the construction of the law." Finlay J.[50] carefully traced the history of the *stare decisis* issue in New Zealand. He seemed reluctant to depart from *Young,* but at the same time seemed willing to broaden the *"per incuriam* exception" to include errors in law! Cornish J.[51] was more forthright:

> As a decisive majority of the two Divisions of this Court think that *In re Houghton, McClurg v. New Zealand Insurance Co., Ltd.* should not be followed, I can see no objection to their not following it. After all, the matter is only one of practice; and I can see no reason (other than *stare decisis*) why both Divisions, if satisfied that a judgment of one Division is not in the true line of authority, should not decline to be bound by it. Any other course would impose on litigants a burden either of expense or delay (or both) of carrying to the Privy Council an appeal which the majority of all the Judges of the Supreme Court and Court of Appeal in this Dominion thought they ought not to carry. It is fairer that the burden of an appeal to the Privy Council should be on the party who seeks to uphold a decision that the two Divisions have rejected.

---

[49] *Ibid.* at p. 484 ff.
[50] *Ibid.* at p. 505 ff.
[51] *Ibid.* at p. 509.

Chapter 5

Stare Decisis: Collateral Issues

The foregoing portions of this study have dealt in general terms with the broad question of the extent to which Commonwealth appellate courts regard themselves as bound by their own decisions. This section concentrates on several specific issues that are subsidiary to the main theme. They are as follows: (1) the effect of decisions of different-sized panels; (2) the effect of decisions of "split courts;" (3) the effect when a higher appellate court considers only a part of the judgment of an intermediate appellate court; (4) the effect when an appellate court follows the decision of a court in another jurisdiction, where the latter decision is subsequently overruled; (5) prospective overruling; (6) conflicting prior decisions of the same court; and (7) the nature of *per incuriam*.

Different-Sized Panels

Whether or not the various Commonwealth appellate courts regard themselves as strictly bound by their own decisions, they have often had occasion to consider whether the decision of a larger panel of judges is a "higher" authority than one pronounced by a smaller panel within the same court. There are really two separate concepts to be examined here. One is whether a panel of five, seven, or more judges can, by virtue of their number, overrule a decision of a panel of three judges of the same court. The other is the extent to which the practice has grown up in a particular court, through enactment or mere usage, of expanding the size of the panel for the purpose of reconsidering earlier decisions. The former is a substantive matter while the latter is more procedural in nature. Other aspects of the question touched on in this section are: (1) the effect of having different divisions of the same court; (2) special situations involving interlocutory matters in appellate courts;

and (3) the binding effect of decisions of one appellate judge.

The issue of numbers takes on more meaning when one considers that in Ontario, for example, a decision of two members of the Court of Appeal could bind the fourteen-member Court.

In the early case of *R. v. Hartfeil,*[1] the Appellate Division of the Alberta Supreme Court listed as one of several reasons for refusing to follow a recent decision of its own the fact that when a panel of five is involved, "there should be less hesitation in overruling a previous decision of three Judges . . . ."

The early English Court of Appeal cases suggested that a larger panel could overrule a smaller one. In *Kelly & Co. v. Kellond*[2] Lord Esher M.R.[3] stated as follows:

> This Court is one composed of six members, and if at any time a decision of a lesser number is called in question, and a difficulty arises about the accuracy of it, I think this Court is entitled, sitting as a full Court, to decide whether we will follow the decision arrived at by the smaller number.

As noted in an earlier section, this view was adopted by the Court in *Re Shoesmith.*[4] However these decisions were criticised in *Young v. Bristol Aeroplane Co., Ltd.*[5] where Lord Greene M.R.[6] observed as follows:

> . . . [W]e can find no warrant for the argument that what is conveniently but inaccurately called the full court has any greater power in this respect than a division of the court consisting of three members only.
>
> The Court of Appeal is a creature of statute and its powers are statutory. It is one court though it usually sits in two or three divisions. Each division has co-ordinate jurisdiction, but the full court has no greater powers or jurisdiction than any division of the court. . . . Neither in the Statute itself nor (save in two cases mentioned hereafter)

---

[1] [1920] 3 W.W.R. 1051 at pp. 1057-8 (Alta. A.D.). Similarly, in *Forsyth v. Forsyth* (1965), 54 W.W.R. 577 at p. 579 Davey J.A. observed that the British Columbia Court of Appeal "has assumed the power to overrule through a division of five judges its previous decisions, if convinced that they were wrongly decided." However, see *R. v. Glenfield,* [1934] 3 W.W.R 465 in which the Appellate Division of the Alberta Supreme Court seemed to question this approach.

[2] (1888), 20 Q.B.D. 569, affirmed *sub nom. Thomas v. Kelly* 13 App. Cas. 506.

[3] *Ibid.* at p. 572.

[4] [1938] 2 K.B. 637 at p. 644.

[5] [1944] K.B. 718.

[6] *Ibid.* at pp. 725, 728.

in decided cases is there any suggestion that the powers of the Court of Appeal sitting with six or nine or more members are greater than those which it possesses when sitting as a division with three members . . . Certainly it cannot be said that there is any statutory right of appeal from a decision of the Court of Appeal to the full court, although on occasions where there has been a conflict caused by the existence of inconsistent earlier decisions the court has ordered the case to be argued before a full court.

Lord Greene M.R. did concede that in cases of this latter kind, "the decision of the full court would be likely to carry greater weight than that of a division of the court." The attitude of the Court of Appeal towards different-sized panels was endorsed by Viscount Simon in the House of Lords.[7] Ironically, Edmund Davies L.J., who felt disposed to follow *Young* in *Barrington v. Lee,*[8] seemed to be influenced by the fact that *Young* itself was the decision of a six-judge court!

In *R. v. Taylor*[9] the fact that a prior decision was being overruled by a unanimous "full court of seven judges" was specifically mentioned in the reasons. However, the overriding consideration was probably the fact that the liberty of the subject was involved. In *R. v. Newsome,*[10] Widgery L.J., after observing that sentencing is "a matter of discretion peculiar to the criminal division," outlined the "restricted sphere" in which the decision of a larger panel would carry more weight:

> . . .[I]f the court of five is duly constituted to consider an issue of discretion and the principles upon which discretion should be exercised, that court ought to have the right to depart from an earlier view expressed by the court of three, especially where that earlier view is very recent and especially where it was a matter in which the court did not have the opportunity of hearing argument on both sides.

Returning to the civil side, the recent case of *Tiverton Estates Ltd. v. Wearwell Ltd.*[11] supports the *Young* rule that decisions of larger panels of the English Court of Appeal enjoy no greater

---

[7] [1946] A.C. 163 at p. 169. This is the prevailing view in the Appellate Division of the Supreme Court of South Africa: see *Fellner v. Min. of the Interior,* [1954] 4 S.A. 524 (A.D.) where it was said that the authority of a decision rests on the status of the Court and not on a counting of heads.

[8] [1971] 3 W.L.R. 962 at p. 974.

[9] [1950] 2 K.B. 368 at p. 371.

[10] [1970] 2 Q.B. 711 at p. 717.

[11] [1974] 2 W.L.R. 176 at p. 196. See also the important recent case of *Davis v. Johnson,* [1978] 2 W.L.R. 553.

authority than panels of three. In at least one instance, this rule
was taken to its most extreme limit. In *Hanning v. Maitland
(No. 2)*[12] a three-judge panel seriously criticized, and perhaps
even overruled, the decision of a five-member Court of Appeal
in *Nowotnik v. Nowotnik.*[13]

In Australia, it seems clear that one aspect of appellate courts'
freedom to overrule themselves is that a larger panel can
overrule a smaller panel in the same court. In the High Court of
Australia case of *Cain v. Malone,*[14] Latham C.J.[15] stated that "a
decision of three Justices . . ., especially with one Justice
dissenting, can certainly be overruled by a Bench of five
Justices." In the Western Australia case of *Kavanaugh v.
Claudius*[16] it was said that a decision of a court of fewer than
four members (four being the normal Full Court) could be
overruled by the Court sitting as a Full Court. Actually, in that
case, a "Full Court" of three overruled a decision of two judges.
In the Queensland case of *R. v. Kaporonowski*[17] it was suggested
that a Court of five judges could not disregard a previous
decision of the Court of Criminal Appeal on a question of
interpretation of a section of *The Criminal Code,* as distinct
from a point of procedure or the exercise of a discretion.

As noted in an earlier section, the Full Court of Appeal in New
Zealand has jurisdiction to overrule the previous decision of one
Division of the Court.[18]

Quite apart from the statements in the cases to the effect that
larger panels of the same appellate court may or may not carry
more weight, there have been some interesting procedural
developments surrounding the practice of increasing the size of
the panel for the purpose of reconsidering a prior decision. Such
procedural innovations may take statutory form, such as the
rather extreme provision in the State of Georgia[19] to the effect
that unanimous decisions by a full bench cannot be overruled or
materially qualified except by a like occurrence. As will be seen,
most developments in Commonwealth jurisdictions are the result
of custom and usage.

---

[12] [1970] 1 All E.R. 812.
[13] [1967] P. 83. In *Ex. p. Yuen Yick Jun,* [1940] 2 D.L.R. 432, a criminal case, a three-member
panel of the B.C. Court of Appeal overruled a previous decision of that court sitting as a five-
member panel.
[14] (1942), 66 C.L.R. 10.
[15] *Ibid.* at p. 15.
[16] (1907), 9 W.A.L.R. 55 (W.A. Sup. Ct. F.C.).
[17] [1972] Q.L.R. 465, per Skerman J. at p. 481.
[18] See *Re Rayner,* [1948] N.Z.L.R. 455, per Finlay J. at p. 505.
[19] Ga. Code Ann. s. 6-1611 (1935).

The use of full courts in the House of Lords has been a relatively rare occurrence.[20] *Jones v. Secretary of State for Social Services*[21] marked only the third time in fifteen years that the House of Lords adjourned a hearing to enable a full court of seven lords to be convened. In *Jones* it was done for the purpose of hearing argument as to whether the House should depart from a previous decision. Shortly after this particular adjournment, the House of Lords issued a practice direction[22] on the procedure to be followed if a party intended to ask the House to depart from a previous decision. It reads as follows:

> If the parties intend to invite the House to depart from one of its own decisions, this must be clearly stated in a separate paragraph of the case, to which special attention must be drawn. The intention must also be restated as one of the reasons.

It seems reasonable to assume that the House of Lords will consider convening a special panel of seven in cases where it appears that its prior decisions will be challenged.[23]

The practice of convening larger panels for this purpose is not unknown in the English Court of Appeal. In *Berkeley v. Papadoyannis*[24] a three-judge Court of Appeal adjourned the case so it could be reargued before a five-judge Court when it seemed apparent (from the notice of appeal) that a previous decision of the Court of Appeal would be challenged on the ground that it had been decided *per incuriam*. Similarly, a five-judge panel was constituted in *Morelle, Ltd. v. Wakeling,*[25] apparently to deal with the previous authority of *Morelle, Ltd. v. Waterworth.*[26] Out of twenty-seven "full court" (seven-judge) decisions of the Court of Criminal Appeal between 1951 and

---

[20] On this topic see L.J. Blom-Cooper and Gavin Drewry, "Full Courts in the Appellate Process" (1971), 34 Mod. L.R. 364.

[21] [1972] A.C. 944.

[22] *Practice Direction (House of Lords: Preparation of Case)*, [1971] 1 W.L.R. 534.

[23] This, however, was not done in the three clear cases in which the House of Lords refused to follow prior decisions: *British Railways v. Herrington*, [1972] 1 All E.R. 749, *The Johanna Oldendorff*, [1973] 3 All E.R. 148, and *Miliangos v. George Frank (Textiles) Ltd.*, [1975] 3 W.L.R. 758.

[24] [1954] 2 Q.B. 149. And see the suggestions of F.J. Odgers in a case comment in (1976), 92 L.Q.R. 321 at p. 323.

[25] [1955] 2 Q.B. 379.

[26] [1955] 1 Q.B. 1. A hearing by a full court has been granted following an undertaking that the appellant would not proceed further to the House of Lords: *Ward v. James*, [1966] 1 Q.B. 273 at p. 279.

1966, at least eleven were convened because of an awkward previous decision of the Court.[27]

The practice of convening larger panels in order to reconsider prior decisions is of course well established in Australia.[28] In a recent case[29] in which the High Court considered whether the Court ought to continue to be bound by Privy Council decisions in view of the limitations on the right of appeal to that court, Barwick C.J.[30] stated that such a question was one of "judicial policy" upon which the Court *as a whole* should pronounce.

In the New Zealand case of *Re Rayner*[31] Fair J.,[32] in the course of criticizing *Young's Case* in the English Court of Appeal, described a novel procedural device available in New Zealand at that time:

> It seems that there should be a means of correcting a decision which is obviously erroneous, even at the possible risk of such power involving uncertainty in the construction of the law.
>
> Furthermore, the position of two Divisions sitting together in New Zealand is markedly different from that of two Divisions sitting together in England. Our Judicature Amendment Act, 1913, in s.9 makes special provision for the two Divisions sitting together on the authority of the Governor-in-Council upon the certificate of two Judges, of whom the Chief Justice shall be one, that any appeal or other proceeding is of special difficulty or importance. That appears to be a statutory recognition of the added weight attributable to decisions of a Court so constituted, and, in itself, to establish a clear difference between the position of our Court of Appeal and that in England.

It does appear, however, that a later amendment[33] has done away with this procedure, or at least the statutory authority for it, though the matter is not entirely free from doubt.

One theme which occasionally emerges in some of the Commonwealth cases in which divisions of appellate courts are combined, or larger panels formed, is whether the new bench so

---

[27] See G. Zellick, "Precedent in the Court of Appeal, Criminal Division," [1974] Crim. L.R. 222 at pp. 223-4.

[28] See, for example, *Australian Agricultural Company et al. v. Federated Engine-Drivers and Firemen's Association of Australasia* (1913), 17 C.L.R. 261 (H.C.) where Powers J. referred at pp. 292-3 to constituting "a full court to consider the review of any prior decision" or at least "as full a bench as is available."

[29] *Favelle Mort Ltd. v. Murray* (1976), 50 A.L.J.R. 509.

[30] *Ibid.* at p. 514.

[31] [1948] N.Z.L.R. 455.

[32] *Ibid.* at p. 485.

[33] The Judicature Amendment Act, 1957 (N.Z.).

created should be regarded as the same court or, alternatively, a new, higher, court. It seems clear from the cases referred to above that it is the "same court" which is involved in these situations. One can think of other situations in which different *sections* of the same court would be involved. For example, in *R. v. Newsome*[34] Widgery L.J.[35] commented that the criminal division of the English Court of Appeal was not, at that time, prepared to regard itself as bound by possible *stare decisis* developments in the civil division.

Along these same lines, it is worth noting some of the recommendations contained in The Report on the Attorney General's Committee on the Appellate Jurisdiction of the Supreme Court of Ontario, 1977 and the implications they could have for *stare decisis* in the Ontario Court of Appeal. The Report[36] envisages the splitting of the Court of Appeal into two sections — a General Section "to hear and dispose of appeals in which there is presented for resolution no question of law of on-going public importance" and a Juristic Section "to hear appeals involving questions of law, the decisions upon which will be of importance to the public generally or some segment of the public, as on-going expositions of the law." The latter section would possess a "supervisory review power" over the General Section, exercisable upon application of a party or at the request of the General Section. Appeals could only be brought before the Juristic Section with leave. The Report stresses that there would continue to be only one Court of Appeal; the two Sections would be "invested with identical jurisdiction." Yet there are suggestions that the Juristic Section may in fact take on the character of a higher appellate court:

> It may seem anomalous to suggest that in a one-tiered appellate structure there could be cases where an application for a further hearing by way of review could be made to one section of the court with respect to an appeal decided by the other section; nevertheless, we have thought that there may be some cases, rare though they may be, where such a right should be available.
>
> It is not necessary to particularize all the kinds of cases which would come within the scope of such a review; one example would be where an important point of law first emerged on the argument before the General Section. Another would be where two panels of the General

---

[34] [1970] 2 Q.B. 711.
[35] *Ibid.* at p. 716.
[36] Report at p. 17 ff.

Section had interpreted the same statute differently: in general terms the Juristic Section should have and exercise such a power *whenever the maintenance of consistency and coherence in the law requires its intervention.* [37]

Presumably a determination by a panel of the Juristic Section would bind panels in the General Section in later cases. At the very least, the proposed reforms are somewhat suggestive of the practice in other jurisdictions where Full Courts are specially constituted, in the interests of certainty, to review past decisions of questionable merit, or to choose between conflicting precedents. However one may view the role of the proposed Juristic Section, it seems clear that the authors of the Report contemplated a mechanism by which at least some previous Court of Appeal decisions could be reviewed without the necessity of taking the matter to the Supreme Court of Canada. Further evidence of this is found at pp. 53-4 of the Report where it is proposed that a litigant have direct access to the Court of Appeal when he seeks "to establish that a previous decision of an appellate court in Ontario should not be followed."

Another aspect of the different-sized panel question is the extent to which a normal panel of three is bound by decisions of *smaller* panels hearing interlocutory matters. The question would only arise in the case of appellate courts which regard themselves as bound by their own previous decisions. There are few authorities on this point. In *Boys v. Chaplin* [38] the English Court of Appeal was unanimously of the view that interlocutory appeals heard by two lords justices were not binding on the court. As Lord Denning M.R. [39] expressed it:

> It was an interlocutory appeal, heard by two lords justices only, on the bare question whether there should be leave to amend or not. Such questions are dealt with expeditiously — I might almost say summarily — because they do not usually raise points of great moment. On the occasions when they do raise important points, arrangements are made to have them heard by three judges.

---

[37] *Ibid.* at p. 20 (emphasis added).

[38] [1968] 2 Q.B. 1, affirmed on other grounds *sub nom. Chaplin v. Boys,* [1971] A.C. 356. In the earlier case of *Glaskie v. Watkins,* [1927] All E.R. Rep. 579, Atkin L.J. at p. 589 expressed the view that a Court of Appeal consisting of three judges is not entitled to overrule a decision of a Court of Appeal consisting of two judges. No reference was made to this case in *Boys v. Chaplin, supra.* Curiously, this statement of Atkin L.J. was omitted from the King's Bench Division Reports.

[39] *Ibid.* at p. 23.

Diplock L.J.[40] was of the same view, primarily because of the "differences in practice in interlocutory and final appeals to the Court of Appeal [which] detract from the weight to be attached to the reasons given for an interlocutory order of the Court of Appeal." These included the absence of a reasoned judgment by the judge against whose order the appeal was brought; the fact that, by statute, interlocutory appeals were placed in a lower category than final appeals; the fact that the appeal could be heard by only two lords justices; and that lengthy and detailed argument was discouraged, as were further appeals to the House of Lords.

A somewhat similar question is that of the binding effect of a decision of a single appellate judge upon a larger panel of judges. Again, there are few appellate courts aside from the Courts of Appeal of England and Ontario where the issue would arise. Decades ago, the issue in England was the binding effect of a decision of the Lord Chancellor alone. It was held that his decision was not absolutely binding on the Court of Appeal[41] and that his prior decision was liable to be reheard.[42] There were views expressed to the contrary, however.[43] After a full discussion of the authorities, Vaughan Williams L.J. concluded in *Re Lloyd*[44] that the Court of Appeal was not so bound.

For some time in Ontario, an appeal from the decision of a Small Claims Court judge could be heard by a single judge of the Court of Appeal. *Bata v. City Parking Canada Ltd.*[45] was such a decision of a single appellate judge. The case was subsequently considered by three-judge panels in the Court of Appeal in *Heffron v. Imperial Parking Co. et al.*[46] and *Trivett v. City Parking Canada Limited.*[47] While it is clear that the Court of Appeal in these later cases disposed of *Bata* on the basis of different facts, Estey J.A. (as he then was) in *Heffron* and Blair J.A. in *Trivett* both alluded to the fact that *Bata* was the decision of a single judge. Significantly, Estey J.A. did refer to the judgment of Schroeder J.A. sitting alone in *Bata,* as "a recent decision *of this Court.*"

---

[40] *Ibid.* at pp. 35-36.
[41] *Wheeldon v. Burrows* (1879), 12 Ch. D. 31.
[42] *Ashworth v. Munn* (1880), 15 Ch. D. 363.
[43] *Gard v. London (City) Sewers Commrs.* (1885), 28 Ch.D. 486.
[44] [1903] 1 Ch. 385 (during argument).
[45] (1973), 2 O.R. (2d) 446.
[46] (1974), 3 O.R. (2d) 722.
[47] Unreported, Court of Appeal, released December 13, 1976.

Split Courts

It is conceivable that an appellate panel composed of an even number of judges could be evenly split on a point of law. Clearly the lower court's decision would be upheld in such a case, but the question is raised as to the binding effect of the appellate court's decision. The position of the Supreme Court of Canada is that when the Court is equally divided so that the decision appealed against stands unreversed, the result of the case in the Supreme Court affects only the actual parties to the litigation, and the Court, when a similar case is brought before it, is not bound by the result of the previous case.[48] Provincial appellate courts have taken this approach as well.[49]

An early statement of the House of Lords suggested that a decision resulting from the Lords being equally divided was as binding upon the House of Lords as if it had been pronounced *nemine dissentiente.*[50] Lord Wright, in an extra-judicial comment,[51] referred to this rule as "an unfortunate result, without any substantial value". After *The Vera Cruz (No. 2)*[52] there was no doubt that the English Court of Appeal would *not* be bound by a decision in which the Court had been evenly split.

The Vera Cruz (No. 2) rule was also adopted by Dixon C.J. in two High Court of Australia[53] cases.

In addition to "equal splits," there have been instances of what might be termed "mixed splits." It has been held in a South African case that where there is a previous decision of the Appellate Division in which three out of the five judges who sat arrived at the same conclusion, one for reason A, one for reason B, and the third for both these reasons, while the two dissenting

---

[48] *Rider v. Snow (Stanstead Election Case)* (1891), 20 S.C.R. 12; see also *M.N.R. v. The Royal Trust Company*, [1931] S.C.R. 485 where Anglin C.J.C. said at p.489 that such a decision is, nevertheless, entitled to great respect.

[49] See, for example, *Clarkson v. A.-G. Canada* (1889), 16 O.A.R. 202, per Osler J.A. at p. 210; *Driscoll v. Colletti* (1926), 58 O.L.R. 444, per Riddell J.A. at p. 450 ff.; and *Pattison v. Behr*, [1920] 1 W.W.R. 417 (Sask.), per MacDonald J. at p. 421. See *Milne v. Federal Commissioner of Taxation* (1975-76), 133 C.L.R. 526 (H.C.Aust.).

[50] *Beamish v. Beamish* (1861), 9 H.L. Cas. 274, per Lord Campbell L.C. See R.E. Megarry, "Decisions by equally divided courts as precedents" (1954), 70 L.Q.R. 318, 471 for an English view of this question.

[51] "Precedents", (1942), 4 U.T.L.J. at p. 258.

[52] (1884), 9 P.D. 96 at 98 (followed in *Clarkson v. A. G. of Canada* (1889), 16 O.A.R. 202). See also *Hobson v. Sir W.C. Leng & Co.*, [1914] 3 K.B. 1245.

[53] *The State of Tasmania v. The State of Victoria* (1934-35), 52 C.L.R. 157 and *Hughes and Vale Proprietary Limited v. The State of New South Wales* (1952-1953), 87 C.L.R. 49 at p. 72. See also *The State of Western Australia v. Hammersley Iron Proprietary Ltd.* (1969), 120 C.L.R. 74.

judges held that both reasons A and B were bad, there is no room for the application of the *stare decisis* rule in respect of either of those reasons; consequently the Appellate Division is not bound in a subsequent case to regard the *ratio decidendi* of the majority as authoritative.[54]

In the Supreme Court of Canada case of *Ross v. The Queen*[55] Strong C.J. did not feel that he was bound by an earlier decision "for the reason that a majority of the judges composing the court were not of accord on any proposition of law on which the decision of the appeal depended." However, a majority of his court were prepared to regard the earlier case as a precedent, and followed it.

Higher Appellate Court Failing to Deal with All the Reasons of the Intermediate Appellate Court

An interesting question is raised when a higher appellate court, in deciding an appeal, refers to some but not all of the reasons of the intermediate appellate court. Do the reasons of the intermediate appellate court which are left unimpaired remain as a precedent?

The situation envisaged here should be contrasted with the situation where the higher court affirms the decision of the intermediate court but on completely different grounds. It has been held that in a case where the House of Lords did this, it thereby indicated that it disagreed with the reasons of the Court of Appeal, and thus the Court of Appeal was no longer bound by them; the "decision" had been affirmed but not the "judgment."[56]

If a provincial appellate court relies on a particular ground, which is subsequently left untouched by the Supreme Court of Canada, the former is not to be regarded as *dicta* but is still binding authority.[57] Similarly, in the Australian High Court case

---

[54] *Fellner v. Minister of the Interior*, [1954] 4 S.A. 524 (A.D.); see a comment on this case by R.N. Gooderson in (1955), 33 C.B.Rev. 612. For a different variation on this same theme see *Prudential Exchange Company Ltd. v. Edwards*, [1939] S.C.R. 135.

[55] (1895), 25 S.C.R. 564.

[56] *Hack v. London Provident Building Society* (1883), 23 Ch. D. 103 (C.A.).

[57] See, for example, *Schwartz v. Winkler* (1901), 13 Man. R. 493 at p. 505 and *Re Budd* (1958), 24 W.W.R. 383 at p. 384. See also a Note by A.J. Stone in (1960), 38 C.B. Rev. 405, commenting on *Re Massey*, [1959] O.R. 608, wherein Wells J. refused to follow the decision of Roach J.A. in *Re Cox*, [1951] O.R. 205 on the basis that because the Supreme Court of Canada had affirmed the decision on another ground stating that the issue in the Court of Appeal judgment did not fall to be determined by them, accordingly this rendered Mr. Justice Roach's opinion *obiter dictum*.

of *Cock v. Aitken*[58] a previous decision of the High Court, *Cock v. Smith,*[59] was followed, notwithstanding the later decision of the Privy Council, *Smith v. Cock,*[60] reversing the previous judgment of the High Court, as the relevant part of the earlier judgment had not in fact been appealed from.

It has been held that where the House of Lords has disapproved of the reasoning of the Court of Appeal without actually overruling the decision itself, the Court of Appeal judgment remains binding.[61] However, as noted in an earlier section, the English Court of Appeal, faced with an unpopular precedent, has held that it is not bound by its own decisions when they have been disapproved, or doubt has been cast upon them, by the Privy Council, despite the fact that Privy Council decisions are not binding upon the Court of Appeal.[62]

Appellate Court Following a Decision from a Foreign Jurisdiction which is Itself Subsequently Overruled

This study does not attempt to examine the binding effect of decisions of foreign courts. It is, however, useful to look briefly at the cases in which appellate courts in one jurisdiction have followed decisions of foreign appellate courts which have subsequently been overruled, and then have been faced with a choice between following their earlier decision or re-examining the question because of the new developments in the foreign jurisdiction.

The Ontario Court of Appeal decision in *Maskewycz v. Maskewycz*[63] is illustrative. There Arnup J.A.[64] summarized his conclusion on this point as follows:

> The overruling of *Bendall v. McWhirter,* [1952] 2 Q.B. 466, by the House of Lords in the *National Provincial Bank* case requires this Court to re-examine the decisions in Ontario which were founded upon *Bendall v. McWhirter.* It is not a situation where a line of authority has developed in England, which the Courts of Canada may or may not choose to follow (as in *The Queen v. Jennnings,* [1966] S.C.R. 532, and *Ares v. Venner,* [1970] S.C.R. 608, 14 D.L.R. (3d) 4, 73 W.W.R. 347),

---

[58] (1911), 13 C.L.R. 461.

[59] (1909), 9 C.L.R. 773.

[60] [1911] A.C. 317.

[61] *Consett Industrial and Provident Society v. Consett Iron Co.,* [1922] 2 Ch. 135 (C.A.).

[62] *Worcester Works Finance Ltd. v. Cooden Engineering Co. Ltd.,* [1971] 3 All E.R. 708.

[63] (1973), 2 O.R. (2d) 713.

[64] *Ibid.* at p. 739 (emphasis added).

but rather a situation in which the Courts of Ontario have accepted as persuasive a basis for a right which the House of Lords has since declared was erroneous. *We are therefore free to re-examine that right and its basis.*

Significantly, one recommendation of the Report of the Attorney General's Committee on the Appellate Jurisdiction of the Supreme Court of Ontario would allow a direct appeal to the proposed Juristic Section of the Court of Appeal in a situation where "there is conflict between a decision of an appellate court in Ontario and that of an appellate court of another province or between decisions of appellate courts of at least two other provinces."[65]

In the Australian High Court case of *Waghorn v. Waghorn*[66] Dixon J.[67] listed examples of cases in which the High Court had followed the English Court of Appeal and thereby overruled its own earlier decision only to find later that the Court of Appeal decision had been overruled by the House of Lords and the law declared in the sense expressed in the decisions which the High Court had overruled. Dixon J. used these examples to buttress his argument that the High Court should not be too closely tied to English decisions.

In the Victorian case of *Perman v. Maloney*[68] the Supreme Court of Victoria declined to follow its earlier decision which had followed an English decision which, unknown to the Australian Court at the relevant time, had later been overruled.

Prospective Overruling

It is not an aim of this study to attempt a detailed critique of the doctrine or technique of prospective overruling. This topic has received extensive treatment by commentators in several countries,[69] particularly the U.S.A. where the literature is voluminous. This section is limited instead to a brief description of prospective overruling as an alternative approach to *stare*

---

[65] Report at p. 54.

[66] (1942), 65 C.L.R. 289.

[67] *Ibid.* at p. 297.

[68] [1939] V.L.R. 376 (Vic. Sup. Ct.). See also *Re W.H. Eutrope & Sons Pty. Ltd.*, [1932] V.L.R. 124 (Vic. Sup. Ct.).

[69] See, for example, M.L. Friedland, "Prospective and Retrospective Judicial Lawmaking" (1974), 24 U.T.L.J. 170; A.G.L. Nicol, "Prospective Overruling: A New Device for English Courts?" (1976), 39 Mod. L.R. 542; W.W. Schaefer, "The Control of 'Sunbursts': Techniques of Prospective Overruling" (1967), 42 N.Y.U.L.R. 631; M.M. Durgala, "Prospectively Overruling the Common Law", (1962), 14 Syrac. L.R. 53; and the vast number of cases and articles referred to therein.

decisis, a listing of the most common arguments in favour of, and against, the technique, and a description of the limited extent to which prospective overruling has been discussed in Commonwealth cases.

An appellate court prospectively overrules a prior decision when it applies it in the *instant* appeal while stating that it will decline to follow it in *future* appeals. This is contrasted with the traditional approach in the British system of law: when the common law is changed by the courts, it is changed retroactively.

The only real models of the operation of prospective overruling are found in the American jurisdictions. The technique has been used by several states and by the United States Supreme Court. However, one commentator[70] has argued that U.S. courts have generally been rather reluctant to employ the technique since the Supreme Court promulgated it in *Great Northern Railway v. Sunburst Co.*[71] There are no jurisdictions in which it is always used. There must be some justification for limiting the retroactive effect. Needless to say, the reliance interest is clearly recognized by the doctrine. Prospective overruling in a tort area would, for example, afford time for a change in insurance coverage.

Prospective overruling has been a vehicle for the implementation of new policies which need not be retroactive to be effective. The new criminal procedure rules fashioned by the U.S. Supreme Court in the 1960's fall into this category.

When a new rule is applied to future cases only and not to the instant appeal, it is a case of "wholly prospective operation." However, there are other variations. An alternative approach is the *"caveat* system" under which the court merely gives a "warning" that it is reconsidering its position before later overruling it.[72]

Other techniques have involved interaction between the judiciary and the legislature. A novel approach was adopted by the Minnesota Supreme Court in response to the controversy over the immunity of school districts from tort liability.[73] The Court did not allow the immediate litigant to recover, but announced that, subject to any legislative changes, it proposed to abrogate

---

[70] M.M. Durgala, op. cit.

[71] 287 U.S. 358 (1932).

[72] See, for example, *Hare v. General Contract Purchase Corp.,* 249 S.W. 2d 973 (1952); *Robinson v. Means,* 95 S.W. 2d 98 (1936).

[73] See *Spanel v. Mounds View School District* 118 N.W. 2d 795, 803 (1962).

the doctrine of immunity after the adjournment of the next
session of the Minnesota legislature.

In England, prior to the 1966 *Practice Statement*, one
commentator advocated the "Reference to Law Reform
Committee Approach,"[74] a proposal heralded as the only one
preferable to complete abolition of the doctrine of *stare decisis*.
By this proposal, *stare decisis* would be retained but the House of
Lords would be empowered to refer matters to a law reform body
and to ensure that Parliament dealt with them within a certain
time. While it is argued that this approach retains the essential
distinction between judiciary and legislature, it would still
appear that this scheme, and the American variations, come
perilously close to breaking down the division of powers between
the two branches of government.

It is beyond the scope of this study to attempt to analyze the
philosophical arguments advanced for and against prospective
overruling. It will suffice merely to list the most common
arguments on either side, concentrating on those most relevant
to Commonwealth courts.

Arguments in favour of prospective overruling centre around
the certainty criterion; parties arranging their affairs should be
entitled to rely on previous decisions until notice is given that
change is imminent. Of course, a future change in a rule could
still affect parties' pre-established rights unless the operation of
the new rule is geared not to the date of decision, but to the date
of the establishment of the rights.

In some areas, it is convenient to change the rule
prospectively. A change in procedural rules, for example, is
unlikely to prejudice parties whose dispute was resolved
according to the earlier procedure.

The main complaint against prospective overruling,
presumably, is that it amounts to saying that the loser should
have been the winner. "What justice after all is there in
enforcing one last time a rule now considered so unjust that it
will not be enforced in subsequent cases? Surely such a margin of
certainty cannot outweigh the merits of doing justice in the case
immediately at hand."[75] Other arguments against prospective
overruling, themselves not free from criticism,[76] include the
following: (1) the judicial process is geared to producing a

---

[74] Gerald Dworkin, "Stare Decisis in the House of Lords" (1962), 25 Mod. L.R. 163 at p. 178.

[75] Daniel A. Lapres, Comment on *Miliangos v. Geo. Frank (Textiles) Ltd.*, [1975] 3 W.L.R. 758 in (1977), 55 C.B. Rev. 132 at p. 142.

[76] See M.M. Durgala, A.G.L. Nicol, op. cit.

retroactive decision; (2) prospective operation usurps a legislative function; (3) a prospective rule would be a mere dictum; (4) lawyers will hestiate to appeal if they know that their efforts will enure only to the benefit of future litigants; and (5) if prospective overruling is available, it will be used every time a court overrules, whether circumstances warrant it or not.

Recent House of Lords cases[77] have asserted rather forcefully that the prospective overruling device is unavailable in England. The *Practice Statement,*[78] of course, made specific reference to retrospective overruling. Yet the *Practice Statement* itself may be regarded in one sense as a form of prospective overruling. And certainly a case like *Hedley Byrne & Co. Ltd. v. Heller & Partners Ltd.,*[79] where a novel legal proposition was established in *obiter dicta* in direct conflict with previous decisions, had the effect of prospectively overruling those decisions.

Lord Simon, on at least two occasions, has suggested that the courts should adopt the technique of prospective overruling. His comments to this effect in *Jones v. Secretary of State for Social Services*[80] are worth quoting at length:

> I am left with the feeling that, theoretically, in some ways the most satisfactory outcome of these appeals would have been to have allowed them on the basis that they were governed by the decision in *Dowling's* case, but to have overruled that decision prospectively. Such a power — to overrule prospectively a previous decision, but so as not necessarily to affect the parties before the court — is exercisable by the Supreme Court of the United States, which has held it to be based on the common law: see *Linkletter v. Walker* (1965) 381 U.S. 618.
>
> In this country it was long considered that judges were not makers of law but merely its discoverers and expounders. The theory was that every case was governed by a relevant rule of law, existing somewhere and discoverable somehow, provided sufficient learning and intellectual rigour were brought to bear. But once such a rule had been discovered, frequently the pretence was tacitly dropped that the rule was pre-existing: for example, cases like *Shelly's Case* (1581) 1 Co. Rep. 93b, *Merryweather v. Nixan* (1799) 8 Term Rep. 186 or *Priestley v. Fowler* (1837) 3 M. & W. 1 were (rightly) regarded as new departures in the law. Nevertheless, the theory, however unreal, had its value — in

[77] *Birmingham City Corporation v. West Midland Baptist (Trust) Association,* [1970] A.C. 874. per Lord Reid at pp. 898-9; *Aries Tanker Corporation v. Total Transport Ltd.,* [1977] 1 W.L.R. 185, per Lord Simon at p. 194.
[78] [1966] 1 W.L.R. 1234.
[79] [1964] A.C. 465.
[80] [1972] A.C. 944 at pp. 1026-27.

limiting the sphere of lawmaking by the judiciary (inevitably at some disadvantage in assessing the potential repercussions of any decision, and increasingly so in a complex modern industrial society), and thus also in emphasising that central feature of our constitution, the sovereignty of Parliament. But the true, even if limited, nature of judicial lawmaking has been more widely acknowledged of recent years; and the declaration of July 20, 1966, may be partly regarded as of a piece with that process. It might be argued that a further step to invest your Lordships with the ampler and more flexible powers of the Supreme Court of the United States would be no more than a logical extension of present realities and of powers already claimed without evoking objection from other organs of the constitution. But my own view is that, though such extension should be seriously considered, it would preferably be the subject-matter of parliamentary enactment. In the first place, informed professional opinion is probably to the effect that your Lordships have no power to overrule decisions with prospective effect only; such opinion is itself a source of law; and your Lordships, sitting judicially, are bound by any rule of law arising extra-judicially. Secondly, to proceed by Act of Parliament would obviate any suspicion of endeavouring to upset one-sidedly the constitutional balance between executive, legislature and judiciary. Thirdly, concomitant problems could receive consideration — for example, whether other courts supreme within their own jurisdictions should have similar powers as regards the rule of precedent; whether machinery could and should be devised to apprise the courts of the potential repercussions of any particular decision; and whether any court (including an Appellate Committee on your Lordships' House) should sit in banc when invited to review a previous decision.

In *Miliangos v. Geo. Frank (Textiles) Ltd.*[81] Lord Simon, dissenting, stated that he would have been more ready to join with the majority if the decision had prospective effect only. He added:

> One of the several reasons why radical law reform is in general more appropriately carried out by Parliament is that a statute can (and usually does) operate prospectively. I venture once again to plead that consideration should be given to the various forms of prospective overruling, such as obtain in some other common law systems.

The notion of prospective overruling has received virtually no mention in Canadian cases, aside from isolated instances where

---

[81] [1975] 3 W.L.R. 758 at p. 792.

procedural rules have been changed for future cases.[82] In *Mire v. Northwestern Mutual Insurance Co.*,[83] McDermid J.A., dissenting, listed prospective overruling as an alternative to overruling retrospectively or adhering to the doctrine of *stare decisis*.

Conflicting Decisions of the Same Appellate Court

One exception to the basic rule in *Young v. Bristol Aeroplane Co. Ltd.*[84] that the English Court of Appeal is bound by its own prior decisions is that it will not be bound in situations where there are in fact conflicting prior decisions of the Court.[85] Then "the Court is entitled and bound to decide which of two conflicting decisions of its own it will follow." This "exception" warrants a brief discussion, as it is one which will take on more and more importance as conflicting precedents accumulate in many areas of the law.

As might be expected, this "exception" has attracted considerable comment and criticism. On the face of it, the exception makes no provision for finality; accordingly, there should be a fixed rule to the effect that where two decisions conflict, the latter should prevail. Alternatively, it might be argued that the earlier case should be binding authority because in theory the court in the later case had no "jurisdiction" to come to a conflicting conclusion. The solution to the problem probably lies in the fact that when the Court chooses between one of two conflicting decisions, the decision not chosen is effectively overruled and the one chosen becomes the binding precedent. One commentator regards this as a "valuable concession to certainty."[86]

The exception has been put to use in recent decisions of the English Court of Appeal. In *A/S Cathrineholm v. Norequipment Trading Ltd.*[87] Roskill L.J. noted that:

> The recent authorities on the question to which this appeal gives rise are numerous and unfortunately conflicting. It is clear that in these

---

[82] See for example *Beaver v. The Queen* (1957), 117 C.C.C. 340.

[83] (1971), 23 D.L.R. (3d) 322 at p. 330 (Alta. C.A.).

[84] [1944] K.B. 718 at p. 729.

[85] Of course it goes without saying that the Supreme Court of Canada considers itself free to elect between conflicting decisions. See *Brant Dairy Co. v. Milk Commission of Ontario* (1972), 30 D.L.R. (3d) 559 at p. 587.

[86] Clive M. Schmitthoff, "The Growing Ambit of the Common Law", (1952), 30 C.B. Rev. 48 at p. 54. This article also examines the interesting question of whether a court will be bound by its own decision to the effect that two prior decisions do *not* conflict.

[87] [1972] 1 W.L.R. 1242.

circumstances this court is not only free but is indeed bound to reconsider the matter afresh unfettered by the authorities, but, of course, obtaining such guidance from them as it is able to do.

In *Tiverton Estates Ltd. v. Wearwell Ltd.*[88] all three members of the Court seized upon the *Young* "exception" in order to choose between conflicting prior decisions. Lord Denning M.R.[89] was of the view that the Court, in so doing, was "overriding" the authorities which were rejected.

Clearly, an overly-liberal view of this exception to *Young* could lead to a rather dramatic relaxing of *stare decisis*. *Ross-Smith v. Ross-Smith*[90] was an example of this. There the Court of Appeal treated two previous decisions as in conflict, and overruled the earlier one, while in fact there was no real conflict, and indeed the first decision had been expressly accepted in the second, and carefully distinguished.

In Canada, even before *Young,* there were indications that the existence of conflicting prior decisions would free appellate courts to adopt their own course.[91] After 1944, the appellate courts in Canadian jurisdictions were able to point to *Young* as well. In *Re Goyan*[92] Gibson J.A., speaking for the Court, observed that in view of the conflicting decisions in the Court of Appeal, the Court "should be bound by the most recent." It is unclear whether this was so because the preferred decision was the most recent.[93] In *Woolfrey v. Piche et al,*[94] LeBel J.A., sitting alone on an appeal from a decision of a small claims court, was faced with conflicting decisions of single judges of the Court of Appeal sitting in similar circumstances. Accordingly, he chose to follow one of the two prior decisions. However, he went on to add the following:

> There is authority also for the proposition that where two cases cannot be reconciled, *the more recent and the more consistent with general principles ought to prevail.*

---

[88] [1974] 2 W.L.R. 176. And see *The Nowy Sacz,* [1978] 2 All E.R. 297 (C.A.).

[89] *Ibid.* at p. 185.

[90] [1961] P. 39.

[91] See, for example, Stuart J. in *R. v. Hartfeil,* [1920] 3 W.W.R. 1051 at p. 1056, citing *Newton v. Cowie* (1827), 12 Moore C.P. 457. See also *Fisken v. Meehan* (1877), 40 U.C.Q.B. 146.

[92] [1953] O.W.N. 297.

[93] One commentator implies that the result reached was correct for the wrong reason: the preferred decision, *Re Gillies,* [1950] O.W.N. 21, was actually a considered *reversal* of the earlier decision, *Re Wright,* [1938] O.R. 117.

[94] (1958), 13 D.L.R. (2d) 605 at p. 608 (emphasis added).

The Nature of Per Incuriam

As is the case with conflicting prior decisions, the *per incuriam* exception to the general rule of *stare decisis* has a direct bearing on the flexibility of that doctrine. Thus it is important to appreciate the essential nature of *per incuriam*. The important authorities in this area are of course decisions of courts such as the English Court of Appeal and the Ontario Court of Appeal, appellate tribunals which have regarded themselves as bound by their own decisions.

In *London Tramways v. L.C.C.*[95] Lord Halsbury expressed the view that a case decided by the House of Lords in ignorance of a statute was one which would not be binding on the House.

The *per incuriam* exception was dealt with as follows by Lord Greene M.R. in *Young v. Bristol Aeroplane Co., Ltd.*:[96]

> . . . Where the court has construed a statute or a rule having the force of a statute its decision stands on the same footing as any other decision on a question of law, but where the court is satisfied that an earlier decision was given in ignorance of the terms of a statute or a rule having the force of a statute the position is very different. It cannot, in our opinion, be right to say that in such a case the court is entitled to disregard the statutory provision and is bound to follow a decision of its own given when that provision was not present to its mind. Cases of this description are examples of decisions given per incuriam. We do not think that it would be right to say that there may not be other cases of decisions given per incuriam in which this court might properly consider itself entitled not to follow an earlier decision of its own. Such cases would obviously be of the rarest occurrence and must be dealt with in accordance with their special facts.

Any suggestion that *per incuriam* was limited to situations in which statutory provisions alone had been overlooked soon fell by the wayside. Clearly the exception was applied as well to cases in which binding authorities had been missed. In *Police Authority for Huddersfield v. Watson*[97] Lord Goddard C.J. had this to say:

---

[95] [1898] A.C. 375 at p. 380.

[96] [1944] 1 K.B.718 at p. 729. See also *Lancaster Motor Co. (London) Ltd. v. Bremith,* [1941] 2 All E.R. 11 in which Lord Greene described a prior decision "delivered without argument and delivered without reference to the crucial words of the rule [of the Supreme Court] and without any citation of authority."

[97] [1947] K.B. 842 at p. 847. See also *R. v. Northumberland Compensation Appeal Tribunal,* [1952] 1 K.B. 338 at p. 343.

What is meant by giving a decision *per incuriam* is giving a decision when a case or statute has not been brought to the attention of the court and it has given its decision in ignorance or forgetfulness of the existence of that case or statute.

A frequently-quoted definition is that of Lord Evershed M.R. in *Morrelle Ltd. v. Wakeling:*[98]

> As a general rule the only cases in which decisions should be held to have been given *per incuriam* are those of decisions given in ignorance or forgetfulness of some inconsistent statutory provision or of some authority binding on the court concerned, so that in such cases some feature of the decision or some step in the reasoning on which it is based is found on that account to be demonstrably wrong. This definition is not necessarily exhaustive, but cases not strictly within it which can properly be held to have been decided *per incuriam*, must, in our judgment, consistently with the *stare decisis* rule which is an essential part of our law, be of the rarest occurrence.

Presumably a failure to cite authority which would not bind the court in any event is insufficient to render a decision one given *per incuriam*; in other words, a later court may decide that the prior defect did not affect the result.

Needless to say, the existence of the *per incuriam* exception often gives rise to somewhat unreal inquiries, often speculative, as to the extent of the material before the court which decided the prior case. The quality of the reporting[99] and recording, and the extent to which authorities and citations are set forth in reasons for judgment, thus become important considerations. This perhaps unfortunate state of affairs has given rise to an evidentiary rule to the effect that a party alleging that a decision is *per incuriam* has the onus of proving his allegation.[100]

Certain situations will not fall into the *per incuriam* category. "That label is relevant only to the right of an appellate court to decline to follow one of its *own* previous decisions, not to its right

---

[98] [1955] 2 Q.B. 379 at p. 406.

[99] For a discussion of the problem of unreported Court of Appeal decisions in this context see A.L. Goodhart, "Precedents in the Court of Appeal" (1945), 9 Cam. L.J. 349 at p. 353. See also the very recent English Court of Appeal decision, *Industrial Properties (Barton Hill) Ltd. v. Associated Electrical Industries Ltd.*, [1977] 2 All E.R. 293, in which the Court declined to follow an earlier decision of its own which was decided on the basis of an incomplete report of an earlier authority.

[100] *Gibson v. South American Stores (Gath & Chaves) Ltd.*, [1949] 2 All E.R. 985, per Evershed M.R. at p. 996.

to disregard a decision of a higher appellate court. . . ."[101] Furthermore, it has been stated that a decision is not *necessarily* made *per incuriam* where a concession by counsel on a point of law is accepted by the court without further investigation.[102] Where an argument has "been only weakly or inexpertly put forward"[103] or there has been a mere "deficiency of parties,"[104] there will be insufficient grounds for a *per incuriam* argument. It has also been suggested that a decision on the interpretation of a statute given without reference to a common rule of statutory construction may not be said to have been given *per incuriam*.[105]

The same general approach towards *per incuriam* is found in the Ontario cases.[106]

The Ontario Court of Appeal case of *Applebaum v. Gilchrist*,[107] however, contains a rather startling departure from the usual concept of *per incuriam*. The majority, wishing to extend to women the cause of action for loss of consortium, was troubled by an earlier, adverse, Court of Appeal decision[108] which had been followed in several later cases involving related causes of action. Without actually using the words *per incuriam*, the majority, in arriving at the desired result, seemed to seize upon the fact that these later cases had not considered an intervening change in The Married Women's Property Act. The amendment in question could hardly have been said to be determinative of the issue. Indeed, the majority felt compelled to point to other factors such as judicial developments in England and policy considerations. Roach J.A.,[109] dissenting, was not prepared to consider the possibility that the prior decisions had been given *per incuriam*.

A more orthodox approach is found in *Re Metro Toronto &*

---

[101] *Broome v. Cassell & Co.*, [1972] A.C. 1027, per Lord Diplock at p. 1131; see also Lord Hailsham at p. 1054 and Viscount Dilhorne at p. 1107.

[102] *Joscelyne v. Nissen et al.*, [1970] 2 Q.B. 86 at p. 99.

[103] *Ibid.* See also *Morelle, Ltd. v. Wakeling*, [1955] 1 All E.R. 708 at p. 718 and *R. v. Bell* (1977), 15 O.R. (2d) 425, per MacKinnon J.A. at p. 430. Note the different result when no argument (as opposed to a poor argument) is put forth on a particular point.

[104] *Morelle, Ltd. v. Wakeling*, [1955] 1 All E.R. 708 at p. 718.

[105] *Royal Crown Derby Porcelain Co. Ltd. v. Raymond Russell*, [1949] 2 K.B. 417, [1949] 1 All E.R. 749. See, however, *Dixon v. British Broadcasting Corporation*, [1979] 1 Q.B. 546 (C.A.).

[106] See, for example, *R. v. Eakins*, [1943] O.R. 199, *R. v. Northern Electric Co. Ltd. et al.*, [1955] O.R. 431 at p. 448, and *R. v. McInnis* (1973), 1 O.R. (2d) 1 at p. 11.

[107] [1946] 4 D.L.R. 383, per Robertson C.J.O. at p. 388 and Laidlaw J.A. at p. 403.

[108] *Lellis v. Lambert* (1897), 24 O.A.R. 653.

[109] *Supra*, f.n. 107 at pp. 410-11.

McGuinness Co. [110] where the Ontario Court of Appeal departed from an earlier decision of its own because some relevant pre-confederation legislation, as well as an early case, had not been called to the Court's attention on that earlier occasion. Aylesworth J.A. [111] observed that "even upon the strictest application of well-recognized exceptions to the rule of *stare decisis,* the case ought to be disregarded and I must therefore refuse to consider it of any further authority upon the point in issue". Similarly in *Re Nicholson & Haldimand-Norfolk Police Commrs Bd.* [112] the Ontario Court of Appeal refused to follow a previous decision which it regarded as having been given *per incuriam* "on the basis that a long series of relevant authorities do not appear to have been drawn to the attention of the Court."

In *City of Kitchener v. Weinblatt* [113] the Court of Appeal departed from an earlier unreported decision of its own. It is unclear whether the Court was simply refusing to follow an unpopular precedent, or whether it was seizing upon the *per incuriam* exception. Evans J.A. [114] (as he then was) stated:

> I would certainly not lightly disregard or depart from any *ratio decidendi* of this Court were it not for the fact that the oral unreported judgment above mentioned does not refer to any authorities and in my opinion is not in accord with the long-established authorities to which I have made reference.

If Evans J.A. was suggesting that the mere fact that the prior decision contained no authorities was sufficient by itself to bring it into the realm of *per incuriam,* this case surely represents a broadening of this particular exception. On the other hand, the result might be explained as an example, not of *per incuriam,* but rather of the conflicting decisions exception.

---

[110] [1960] O.R. 267.

[111] *Ibid.* at p. 275.

[112] (1976), 12 O.R. (2d) 337 at p. 351. This decision has since been appealed to the Supreme Court of Canada.

[113] (1966), 58 D.L.R. (2d) 332, affirmed [1969] S.C.R. 157.

[114] *Ibid.* at p. 337.

Chapter 6

The Rationale of Stare Decisis

Earlier sections of this study have examined the extent to which Commonwealth appellate tribunals regard themselves as bound by their own prior decisions. This section of the study attempts a brief listing of the reasons courts have given for supporting the doctrine of *stare decisis*, or departing from it. The various pros and cons will be examined in turn.[1]

Arguments in Support of Stare Decisis

Obviously the main supporting pillar of the *stare decisis* doctrine is the expressed desire for certainty and predictability in the system.[1a] Uncertainty, it is said, is contrary to public policy;[2] to promote uncertainty is to commit a miscarriage of justice.[3]

Significantly, the importance of certainty in the law has been asserted forcefully by the House of Lords in cases decided subsequent to the *Practice Statement.*[4] Certainty, no doubt, was the "intangible" matter of "judicial policy" referred to by Else-Mitchell J. in *Lord v. Still:*[5] it takes on considerable importance "for the maxim stare decisis is not merely a catch phrase but an

---

[1] For a recent comprehensive catalogue of pros and cons in the Australian context, see L.V. Prott, "When Will a Superior Court Overrule Its Own Decisions?" (1978), 52 Aust. L.J. 304; see also C.E.F. Rickett, "Precedent in the Court of Appeal", (1980), 43 Mod. L.R. 136.

[1a] See, for example, *Barnett v. Harrison,* [1976] 2 S.C.R. 531, per Dickson J. at p. 559; *Stuart v. Bank of Montreal* (1909), 41 S.C.R. 516 at pp. 549-50; *Sweney v. The Department of Highways,* [1933] O.W.N. 783 (C.A.), quoting Scrutton L.J. in *Hill v. Aldershot Corporation,* [1933] 1 K.B. 259 at p. 263; *Gallie v. Lee,* [1969] 2 W.L.R. 901 at p. 918 (C.A.).

[2] *Myers v. D.P.P.,* [1965] A.C. 1001, per Lord Reid at p. 1022.

[3] *Delta Acceptance Corporation Ltd. v. Redman,* [1966] 2 O.R. 37, per McGillivray J.A. at p. 42.

[4] See, for example, *Knuller v. D.P.P.,* [1973] A.C. 435, per Lord Reid at p. 455; *Miliangos v. Geo. Frank (Textiles) Ltd.,* [1975] 3 W.L.R. 758, per Lord Cross at p. 797.

[5] [1962] S.R. (N.S.W.) 709 (N.S.W. Sup. Ct. F.C.) at p. 716.

expression of judicial obligation, even if that obligation is of a fluctuating character."

One approach in this area stresses the inconvenience of uncertainty. The classic statement is that of Halsbury L.J. in *London Street Tramways v. L.C.C.*:[6]

> Of course I do not deny that cases of individual hardship may arise, and there may be a current of opinion in the profession that such and such a judgment was erroneous; but what is that occasional interference with what is perhaps abstract justice, as compared with the inconvenience — the disastrous inconvenience — of having each question subject to being re-argued and the dealings of mankind rendered doubtful by reason of different decisions, so that in truth and in fact there would be no real final court of appeal. My Lords, 'interest rei publicae' that there should be 'finis litium' sometime and there could be no finis litium if it were possible to suggest in each case that it might be re-argued because it is 'not an ordinary case' whatever that may mean.

Duff J. in *Stuart v. Bank of Montreal*[7] referred to "principles of public convenience too obvious to require statement". In the same case Anglin J.[8] expressed his fear that there would be a loss of respect for judgments if the doctrine of *stare decisis* were not followed.

As Lord Halsbury suggested in *London Street Tramways*, certainty is often equated with finality of litigation, itself a desirable feature of the system.[9] In *Jones v. Secretary of State for Social Services*,[10] Lord Reid[11] expressed his fear that a departure from precedent in that case would encourage litigants to think that the old rules no longer barred the path in other areas of the law. One theme which appears in the older cases particularly is that departures from precedent would "encourage a race," that is, "forum-shopping" would become the norm if courts of coordinate jurisdiction were not bound.[12] As Hutley A.J.A. put it in *Flanagan v. H.C. Buckman & Son Pty. Ltd.*:[13]

---

[6] [1898] A.C. 375 at p. 380.

[7] (1909), 41 S.C.R. 516 at p. 535, affd. [1911] A.C. 120.

[8] *Ibid.* at p. 550.

[9] See, for example, *Velazquez Ltd. v. Inland Revenue Commissioners*, [1914] 3 K.B. 458, per Lord Cozens-Hardy M.R. at p. 461; *Gallie v. Lee*, [1969] 2 W.L.R. 901 (C.A.), per Russell L.J. at p. 918.

[10] [1972] A.C. 944.

[11] *Ibid.* at p. 966.

[12] See, for example, *Re Hotchkiss's Trusts* (1869), L.R. 8 Eq. 643.

[13] [1972] 2 N.S.W. L.R. 761 at p. 781 (N.S.W. Sup. Ct., C.A.).

[B]attles fought and lost cannot be refought with the same weapons to produce a different result.

The certainty argument would seem to be most forceful when the appellate court is faced with a relatively recent prior decision,[14] though there are certainly numerous cases which take the opposite approach.[15] It is suggested that there is no clear rule in this regard.

Courts have identified certain areas in which the strict application of the doctrine of *stare decisis* is particularly important. Examples include constitutional law,[16] practice,[17] wills[18] and conveyancing.[19]

One of the most frequently-cited reasons for a rigid adherence to *stare decisis* is the importance of preserving existing proprietary or contractual rights.[20] Indeed, it must not be overlooked that the House of Lords *Practice Statement* makes specific reference to "the danger of disturbing retrospectively the basis on which contracts, settlements of property and fiscal arrangements have been entered into . . .". Courts have often stressed their extreme reluctance to interfere with long standing and widely accepted rules of commerce which clearly formed the basis of the contract in question.[21] The same is true of practices which have grown up in the area of company law.[22]

In *Geelong Harbor Trust Commissioners v. Gibbs, Bright & Co.*[23] the court observed.

> The law laid down by a judicial decision, even though erroneous, may work in practice to the satisfaction of those who are affected by it,

---

[14] See, for example, *Barrington v. Lee,* [1971] 3 W.L.R. 962, per Edmund Davies L.J. at p. 974.

[15] See, for example, *Jones v. Secretary of State for Social Services,* [1972] A.C. 944, per Viscount Dilhorne at p. 993: "It is a comparatively recent decision and may not as yet have affected many claims".

[16] See, for example, *Hughes and Vale v. N.S.W.* (1952-53), 87 C.L.R. 49 at pp. 70 ff., 76, 102.

[17] *Clarke v. Huron County Flax Mills* (1922), 51 O.L.R. 560, per Meredith C.J.O. at p. 562; *Whitehead v. City of N. Vancouver,* [1937] 2 W.W.R. 95 at p. 96.

[18] *Re Guthrie* (1924), 56 O.L.R. 189 at p. 196; *Re Whitney* (1970), 13 D.L.R. (3d) 602 at p. 611.

[19] *Caldwell v. McLaren* (1884), 9 App. Cas. 392 at p. 409 (P.C.).

[20] See, for example, *Birmingham City Corporation v. West Midland Baptist (Trust) Association,* [1970] A.C. 874, per Lord Reid at pp. 898-9.

[21] For an excellent example of this, see the recent case of *Aries Tanker Corporation v. Total Transport Ltd.,* [1977] 1 W.L.R. 185 (H.L.); see also *Atlantic Shipping and Trading Co. v. Dreyfus and Co.,* [1922] 2 A.C. 250 at p. 257; with respect to commercial documents see *The Annefield,* [1971] 2 W.L.R. 320, at pp. 331, 333.

[22] *Commonwealth v. Cigamatic Pty. Ltd.* (1962), 108 C.L.R. 372 (H.C.), per McTiernan J. at pp. 380-1.

[23] [1974] A.C. 810 at p. 818-19.

particularly where it concerns the allocation of the burden of unavoidable risks between parties engaged in trade or commerce and their insurers. If it has given general satisfaction and caused no difficulties in practice, this is an important factor to be weighed against the more theoretical interests of legal science in determining whether the law so laid down ought now to be changed by judicial decision.

It has been said that the fact that most actions threatened or begun are settled by agreement is to the great advantage of the public generally and the litigants in particular. Since lawsuits are settled on the basis of a prognostication of the applicable law, it is essential, so the argument goes, that the rules be predictable, especially in the areas in which legal disputes most frequently arise.[24]

Another argument advanced in favour of strict adherence to the doctrine of *stare decisis* is that changing the law by overruling a prior precedent amounts to usurping the role of Parliament.[25] Indeed, Lord Campbell in *Beamish v. Beamish*[26] maintained that it would be unconstitutional for the House of Lords to refuse to be bound by its previous decisions as it would be arrogating to itself the right of altering the law and legislating by its own separate authority. One might wonder how strenuously this argument should be made, as the House of Lords is, to a certain extent, a merger of the legislature and judiciary. In the United States there is a much clearer division of legislative and judicial functions; yet, ironically perhaps, the argument based on the improprietary of judicial legislation is not taken seriously.

The argument based on a supposed usurpation of the role of Parliament is perhaps best demonstrated in cases where the court is confronted with a prior decision construing a statute. It has been forcefully argued that prior decisions on the construction of statutes should only be reconsidered in rare cases.[27] It is said that reform is best left to Parliament by means of amending legislation with prospective effect only.[28] Yet the

---

[24] On this theme see *Farrell v. Alexander*, [1976] 2 All E.R. 721, per Lord Simon at p. 741.

[25] See, for example, *Pettitt v. Pettitt*, [1970] A.C. 777, per Lord Reid at p. 795, and *Hesperides Hotels Ltd. v. Aegean Turkish Holidays Ltd.*, [1978] 3 W.L.R. 378 (H.L.).

[26] (1861), 9 H.L. Cas. 274 at p. 338.

[27] See, for example, *Jones v. Secretary of State for Social Services*, [1972] A.C. 944 per Lord Reid at p. 966.

[28] *Geelong Harbour Trust Commissioners v. Gibbs, Bright & Co.* (1970), 122 C.L.R. 504 (H.C.), per McTiernan and Menzies JJ. at p. 518.

courts have not hesitated to take the opposite approach at times.[29]

A subsidiary argument often advanced in favour of *stare decisis* is that Parliament "had chances to alter the law", but did not do so. This was one approach taken in *Knuller v. D.P.P.*[30] for example, but it is not without its critics, one of whom, significantly enough, was Lord Reid in that same case.[31]

A final argument (where applicable) in favour of *stare decisis* is that there exists a higher appellate court for the purpose of correcting errors. One of the early expressions of this is found in *Taylor v. Burgess*[32] which was decided in an era when there were three courts of coordinate jurisdiction in England with different rights of appeal to the Court of Exchequer Chamber:

> When a case can be taken to a court of error, the decision of one court of coordinate jurisdiction ought to be binding on the others. When, however, there is no means of appealing to a court of error there is not the same obligation to follow the decision of another court . . .

In more recent times, it has often been said in English cases that the availability of the House of Lords to correct error in the Court of Appeal makes its unnecessary for the intermediate appellate tribunal to depart from the principle of *stare decisis*.[33]

Obviously the force of this particular argument will depend in large part upon the nature of the constraints placed upon the right of appeal to a higher tribunal. As has been noted in earlier portions of this study, the placing of elaborate limitations upon parties' rights of appeal has become the norm in recent years in several Commonwealth jurisdictions.

To the extent that higher courts are available to the parties, the system will encourage further litigation. It is well to recall the argument of the proponents of certainty who would stress adherence to *stare decisis* as a means of curbing the proliferation of actions.

---

[29] See, for example, *Concrete Constructions Proprietary Limited v. Barnes* (1938), 61 C.L.R. 209 (H.C.); *Jones v. Secretary of State for Social Services*, [1972] A.C. 944, per Viscount Dilhorne at p. 993: "I see no valid reason for thinking that this House should be especially reluctant to correct an error if the decision thought to be wrong is as to the construction of a statute".

[30] [1973] A.C. 435, per Lord Morris at p. 466. See also *Binus v. The Queen*, [1967] S.C.R. 594, per Cartwright J. at p. 601.

[31] [1973] A.C. 435 at p. 455.

[32] (1859), 5 H. and N. 1, per Pollock C.B. at p. 5.

[33] See, for example, *Gallie v. Lee*, [1969] 2 W.L.R. 901, per Russell L.J. at p. 918; *Tiverton Estates Ltd. v. Wearwell Ltd.*, [1974] 2 W.L.R. 176, per Scarman L.J. at p. 196.

Arguments Against Stare Decisis

The doctrine of *stare decisis* has been attacked from all quarters for practical as well as purely philosophical reasons. Foremost among the latter was Glanville Williams'[34] exposing of the "circularity" argument inherent in the doctrine of *stare decisis*: courts are absolutely bound by their own decisions because this has been stated in other cases which are assumed to be absolutely binding.

For the most part the main arguments against *stare decisis* are simply the converse of the arguments in support of the doctrine. For example, it has been said that to do away with the doctrine would actually promote certainty in the law. In essence, certainty need not be served with exclusivity to be served well. The American jurist, Justice Douglas, articulated this argument very well:

> This search for a static security — in the law or elsewhere — is misguided. The fact is that security can only be achieved through constant change, through the wise discarding of old ideas that have outlived their usefulness, and through the adopting of others to current facts. There is only an illusion of safety in a Maginot Line. Social forces like armies can sweep around a fixed position and make it untenable. A position that can be shifted to meet such forces and at least partly absorb them alone gives hope of security.[35]

Lord Reid adopted a somewhat different variation of this same argument in *Jones v. Secretary of State for Social Services*:[36]

> The old view was that any departure from rigid adherence to precedent would weaken . . . certainty. I did not and do not accept that view. It is notorious that where an existing decision is disapproved but cannot be overruled courts tend to distinguish it on inadequate grounds. I do not think that they act wrongly in so doing: they are adopting the less bad of the only alternatives open to them. But this is bound to lead to uncertainty for no one can say in advance whether in a particular case the court will or will not feel bound to follow the old unsatisfactory

---

[34] In *Salmond on Jurisprudence*, 11th ed.

[35] "Stare Decisis" (1949), 49 Col. L.R. 735 at p. 735. An extreme, and perhaps silly, example is found in *Alferitz v. Borgwardt*, 126 Cal. 201, 208, 58 P. 460, 462 (1899), where a court overruled itself and stated that its earlier decision was so bad that everyone should have known it would be overruled, and that a lawyer who relied on it in advising a client would have demonstrated his incompetence!

[36] [1972] A.C. 944 at p. 966.

decision. On balance it seems to me that overruling such a decision will promote and not impair the certainty of the law . . . But that certainty will be impaired unless this practice is used sparingly.

No doubt with observations like the foregoing in mind, Professor Laskin (as he then was) referred to the "considerations of certainty and predictability of judicial decisions and the reliance on them by the citizenry in their transactions and relationships" mustered in justification of strict adherence to *stare decisis,* as being of a " 'will of the wisp' nature."[37]

Similarly the arguments in favour of *stare decisis* based on the importance of preserving existing property rights are countered with arguments stressing the inevitability of economic and social change. There are several sub-themes here.

First, it is said that courts must avoid the absurdity and injustice that can result when old precedents are applied in modern social contexts. As Lord Denning observed in his dissenting opinion in *London Transport Executive v. Betts:*[38]

> It seems to me that when a particular precedent — even of your Lordships' House — comes into conflict with a fundamental principle, also of your Lordships' House, then the fundamental principle must prevail. This must at least be true when, on the one hand, the particular precedent leads to absurdity or injustice and, on the other hand, the fundamental principle leads to consistency and fairness. It would, I think, be a great mistake to cling too closely to particular precedent at the expense of fundamental principle.

Second, it is said that courts must avoid the charade of distinguishing prior decisions on insufficient grounds.[39] The classic statement is that of Lord Reid in *Nash v. Tamplin:*[40]

> My Lords, it is very unsatisfactory to have to grope for a decision in this way, but the need to do so arises from the fact that this House has debarred itself from ever reconsidering any of its own decisions. It matters not how difficult it is to find the *ratio decidendi* of a previous case, that *ratio* must be found.

---

[37] "The Supreme Court of Canada: A final Court of and for Canadians", (1951), 29 C.B.Rev. 1038 at p. 1072.

[38] [1959] A.C. 213 at p. 247 (H.L.). See also *Birmingham City Corporation v. West Midland Baptist (Trust) Association (Inc.),* [1970] A.C. 874, per Lord Reid at p. 898.

[39] See, for example, *Jones v. Secretary of State for Social Services* [1972] A.C. 944, per Lord Reid at p. 966; *The Johanna Oldendorff,* [1973] 3 All E.R. 148, per Lord Reid at p. 156.

[40] [1952] A.C. 231 at p. 251.

Third, as suggested in the passage from the reasons of Lord Denning quoted *supra*, it is argued that the "development and application of fundamental principles" is conceptually distinct from, and should be preferred to, rigid adherence to prior precedents. As Justice Frankfurter once expressed it:

> We recognize that stare decisis embodies an important social policy. It represents an element of continuity in law, and is rooted in the psychologic need to satisfy reasonable expectations. But stare decisis is a principle of policy and not a mechanical formula of adherence to the latest decision, however recent and questionable, when such adherence involves collision with a prior doctrine more embracing in its scope, intrinsically sounder, and verified by experience.[41]

Similarly Lord Reid stated in *Myers v. D.P.P.*[42] that

> The common law must be developed to meet changing economic conditions and habits of thought, and I would not be deterred by expressions of opinion in this House in old cases. But there are limits to what we can or should do. If we are to extend the law it must be by the development and application of fundamental principles. We cannot introduce arbitrary conditions or limitations: that must be left to legislation. And if we do in effect change the law, we ought in my opinion only to do that in cases where our decision will produce some finality or certainty.

It is useful to take note of a few examples where these approaches have been applied. It will be recalled from earlier portions of this study that the House of Lords in *Miliangos v. Geo. Frank (Textiles) Ltd.*[43] departed from an earlier precedent dealing with the relevant conversion date for the payment of judgments in foreign currency. In that case Lord Wilberforce stated:

> . . . if I am faced with the alternative of forcing commercial circles to fall in with a legal doctrine which has nothing but precedent to commend it or altering the doctrine so as to conform with what commercial experience has worked out, I know where my choice lies. The law should be responsive as well as, at times, enunciatory, and good doctrine can seldom be divorced from sound practice.[44]

---

[41] In *Helvering v. Hallock*, 60 Sup. Ct. 444 (1940), at p. 450.

[42] [1965] A.C. 1001 at p. 1021. See also Professor J. Stone's "three phases of overruling" described in "On the Liberation of Appellate Judges", (1972) 35 Mod. L.R. 449 at pp. 471-3.

[43] [1975] 3 W.L.R. 758.

[44] *Ibid.* at p. 768.

In the same case, Lord Edmund-Davies[45] was "glad" that the social circumstances had so greatly changed since the earlier precedent was decided that the court could "avoid perpetrating the great injustice which would result were the *ratio decidendi* of that case applied to the present claim."

In *British Railways Board v. Herrington,*[46] an occupier's liability case, an earlier precedent was discarded because it had "been rendered obsolete by changes in physical and social conditions," and had become "an incumbrance impeding the proper development of the law." And, as noted in an earlier section of this study, the English Court of Appeal in the recent cases of *Cooke v. Head*[47] and *Dyson Holdings Ltd. v. Fox*[48] departed from precedent in order to give effect to changing social attitudes toward "common-law" marriages.

The argument in favour of *stare decisis,* to the effect that a departure from precedent amounts to a usurpation of the role of Parliament, is countered with the argument that Parliament cannot effectively legislate in some areas, and, indeed, that some areas are not proper ones for legislative reform.

In the *Miliangos*[49] case, Lord Wilberforce observed:

> . . .[F]rom some experience in the matter, I am led to doubt whether legislative reform, at least prompt and comprehensive reform, in this field of foreign currency obligation, is practicable. Questions as to the recovery of debts or of damages depend so much upon individual mixtures of facts and merits as to make them more suitable for progressive solutions in the courts.

In this regard, courts have often expressed their doubts as to whether Parliament has sufficient time to devote to the reform of rather narrow, specific rules of private law. As Russell L.J. remarked in *Gallie v. Lee:*[50]

> In the case of decisions of the House of Lords error, or what is later considered to be error, could only previously be corrected by statute: and the other demands on parliamentary time made this possibility so

---

[45] *Ibid.* at p. 802. See also *The Johanna Oldendorff,* [1973] 3 All E.R. 148 at p. 155.

[46] [1972] 1 All E.R. 749 (H.L.), especially at p. 785 ff.

[47] [1972] 2 All E.R. 38.

[48] [1975] 3 All E.R. 1030.

[49] [1975] 3 W.L.R. 758 at p. 773. And see Iain Ramsay, "Miliangos v. George Frank Textiles (Ltd.) and the Role of the Judicial Process in the Reform of the Common Law", (1977), 15 U.W.O.L.Rev. 213.

[50] [1969] 2 W.L.R. 901 at p. 918, affd. *sub. nom. Saunders v. Anglia Building Society,* [1971] A.C. 1004. See also Viscount Dilhorne in *Davis v. Johnson,* [1978] 1 All E.R. 1132 at p. 1146.

remote that the decision of the House of Lords not neccessarily to be bound by a previous decision was justifiable at the expense of some loss of certainty.

Of course there may be areas, such as the division of powers under a constitution for example, where Parliament is not in a position to change the law. Accordingly courts must be free to re-examine prior decisions in these areas if the rules are to respond to social change.[51]

Finally, it is said that *stare decisis* should not be adhered to too rigidly when the court involved is in fact the final available appellate court; the ultimate court of appeal should be free to exercise its "independent judgment" in every case.[52] It has also been argued that an intermediate appellate court should be free to regard *itself* as a final court of appeal *in effect,* where there are substantial limitations upon the right of appeal to the *actual* court of last resort, or where distance, delay and expense make appeals to the latter impractical.[53]

---

[51] See a discussion of this in *Perpetual Executors & Trustees Association of Australia Ltd. v. Commissioner of Taxation* (1949), 77 C.L.R. 493 (H.C.).

[52] See, for example, *The Canadian Bank of Commerce v. Perram* (1899), 31 O.R. 116; *Mercier v. Campbell* (1907), 14 O.L.R. 639, at pp. 644-5; *Crowe v. Graham* (1910), 22 O.L.R. 145; *Farrell v. Gallagher* (1911), 23 O.L.R. 130 at p. 136; and *Re Ryley Hotel Co. Ltd.* (1910), 15 W.L.R. 229 at p. 236.

[53] As to the latter, see *Re Rayner,* [1948] N.Z.L.R. 455 at p. 485. See also the comments of Lord Salmon in *Davis v. Johnson,* [1978] 1 All E.R. 1132 at p. 1153.

Chapter 7

Conclusion

_____

While Commonwealth appellate courts of last resort are now unanimous that they are free to depart from their previous decisions, the matter remains controversial among intermediate appellate courts. For example, the English Court of Appeal on several occasions[1] has refused to follow its previous decision, only to be upbraided by the House of Lords,[2] while in contrast, the Ontario Court of Appeal has consistently refused to depart from its previous decisions to which the Supreme Court of Canada has responded in a decidedly "hands-off" manner.[3]

The position taken by the House of Lords is conceptually puzzling if not logically confused.[4] It would have been nonetheless remarkable had it confined itself to a gratuitous observation of the position which in its opinion the Court of Appeal should take, but it did not so restrict itself. In *Davis v. Johnson,*[5] Lord Diplock directly stated that the question before the House for decision was "whether [the Court of Appeal] was bound by its own previous decisions," and concluded:

In my opinion, this House should take this occasion to re-affirm expressly,

_____

[1] A considerable number of such cases are reviewed by Denning M.R. in *Davis v. Johnson* [1978] 1 All E.R. 841 at 856. See also the discussion supra at Chap. 2 page 8-10.

[2] *Davis v. Johnson,* [1978] 1 All E.R. 1132.

[3] *Bell v. The Queen* (1979), 98 D.L.R. (3d) 255 per Spence, J. at p. 261.
    See G. Bale, "Casting Off the Mooring Ropes of Binding Precedent" (1980), 58 C.B. Rev. 255 at p. 273.

[5] [1978] 1 All E.R. 1132.

unequivocally and unanimously that the rule laid down in the *Bristol Aeroplane* case as to *stare decisis* is still binding on the Court of Appeal.[6]

Following Lord Diplock's suggestion, the House of Lords was unanimous in its rebuke, and almost unanimous in its purported adjudication. All but Lord Salmon concurred in Lord Diplock's 'ruling of law' on the point. Lord Salmon appeared to follow suit but then, as one commentator has observed, "gave the show away by tacitly admitting the faulty logic of the position adopted by the House of Lords."[7] While Lord Salmon three times in his judgment states that he agrees with the opinion of the other Law Lords that the Court of Appeal is bound by its own previous decisions, in virtually the same breath he adds:

> In the nature of things however, the point could never come before Your Lordships' House for decision or form part of its *ratio decidendi*. This House decides every case that comes before it according to the law. If, as in the instant case, the Court of Appeal decides an appeal contrary to one of its previous decisions, this House, much as it may deprecate the Court of Appeal's departure from the rule, will nevertheless dismiss the appeal if it comes to the conclusion that the decision appealed against was right in law.[8]

It has already been observed that the principle of *stare decisis* derives its authority not from some external source, but as a matter of practice, courtesy, or what might be termed "internal discipline" on the ground of judicial comity.[9] But as one U.S. jurist aptly stated: "Comity persuades; but it does not command."[10] Absent external authority the principle governs only those who submit, for it is a rule without a sanction.[11] As such, it can be altered without the intervention of superior

---

[6] *Ibid.* at p. 1139-40. Interestingly , some years before, extrajudicially, Lord Diplock, "suggested . . . that obscurity and complication . . . in some branches of the law, are the product of the past failure of the Courts to act with courage when it became apparent that a rule of conduct laid down in earlier decisions had become out of date." He went on to recall "the bold imaginative judgments delivered by a great generation of judges between the sixties and the nineties of the last century" and lamented that "somehow, at the turn of the century the Courts seemed to have lost their courage. In the clash between precedent and flexibility precedent seemed to win the day." Lord Diplock, "The Courts as Legislators," an address delivered at The University of Birmingham, Holdsworth Club, on March 26, 1965 pp. 18, 20, 21.

[7] *Supra,* f.n. 4 at p. 273.

[8] *Supra,* f.n. 5 at p. 1152.

[9] *Supra,* at p. 2-3.

[10] *Mast, Foos & Co. v. Stone Mfg. Co.,* 177 U.S. 485 at 488 (7th cir., 1900).

[11] For a rare instance of judicial elaboration upon the point see the judgment of Matheson Co. Ct. J. in *R. v. Beaney* (1969), 4 D.L.R. (3d) 369 at 374.

authority as was done by the House of Lords in its Practice Statement of 1966, and somewhat less theatrically by the Supreme Court of Canada in *R. v. Paquette*[12] and *McNamara Construction (Western) Limited v. The Queen.*[13] Yet if the matter is one of practice or internal discipline, one wonders what authority a superior court could call upon to justify its intrusion into the internal discipline of the lower court and its insistence that the judicial function of that court can only be properly discharged by observing strict adherence to the rule of *stare decisis*: all the more so when that superior court acknowledges that in discharging its own duty, it is not so bound and indeed is compelled to conclude in accordance with the requirements of law and justice.

The insistence on strict observance of the principle of *stare decisis* has itself been deprecated as "arrogant and presumptuous" because it is "an attempt to bind later courts."[14] The point would have greater force if observance of the doctrine were not a matter of voluntary submission. However, if the authority of the rule (as residing solely in voluntary submission) becomes obscured and judges assume, as the House of Lords has purported to direct, that the rule stands on some higher authority, then the criticism of arrogance and presumptuousness may more properly be advanced. So long as judges, in observing or declining to observe strict application of *stare decisis* on a case-by-case basis, do so on the basis of a reasoned decision, they are neither abdicating their function to a rule, nor permitting their function to be abrogated by the decisions of their predecessors. But should judges observe strict adherence to the rule on the assumption that it has authority beyond the individual considerations which they consider commends it to them in the particular case, there is both abdication and abrogation of the judicial function; and this is precisely what the House of Lords in *Davis v. Johnson* not just invites, but purports to command.

What then are the considerations which might lead a jurist to conclude that strict application of the principle of *stare decisis* is the best compromise of conflicting values? The arguments most often advanced in support of maintaining strict adherence are those asserting the need for certainty, predictability and propriety in the law. That view was recently expressed by Evans

---

[12] (1976), 30 C.C.C. (2d) 417.
[13] [1977] 2 S.C.R. 654.
[14] *Supra*, f.n. 4 at p. 103.

J.A. (as he then was) in *Engler v. Rossignol,*[15] when he observed:
"Uniformity is much more desirable for the litigant than the
uncertainty of judicial creativity."

The arguments for and against certainty and predictability
have already been canvassed. It may be that when one raises
these arguments in defence of the doctrine one has in mind cases
of a special type in which the reliance interest is strongest, such
as matters of conveyance where the validity of titles rests upon a
previous decision, or matters of contract where commercial
affairs have been arranged in reliance on the law as stated. That
courts recognize these interests, even when not bound by judicial
authority, is beyond question; the argument for protection of
such interests would seem to be much stronger when it arises
from a previous decision of the court.

Yet if the argument for strict adherence rests solely upon the
protection of people's reliance on former decisions, then in view
of the court's recognized ability to protect that interest in other
circumstances where there exists no rule compelling such, it
would seem to be an unnecessary fetter of judicial function to
impose strict adherence regardless of whether or not a reliance
interest is present. If the court is capable of adequately
protecting that interest without an absolute rule in cases where
there is no previous decision, then it ought to be equally capable
of protecting it without the need for such a rule in cases where
there is a previous decision.

A related and perhaps emotionally more compelling
argument for maintaining strict adherence to *stare decisis* is
founded upon a demand for propriety in the law. The argument
claims its foundation in the rule that every man stands equal
before the law. It is a fundamental tenet of the common law and
the English system of justice that like cases are to be decided
alike. The argument insists that while one may be willing to
sacrifice a litigant's reliance upon a previous decision where that
is the only aspect of his case which commends itself, one may be
less willing to sacrifice the integrity of the law by affording one
litigant a different result from that permitted a previous litigant.
No doubt it was this apparent impropriety which McGillivray
J.A. had in mind in *Delta Acceptance Corp. Ltd. v. Redman*
when he stated that for the court to fail to recognize the
plaintiff's reliance interest as determinative in that case "would
be a miscarriage of justice."[16] But whether it is certainty or

---

[15] (1975), 10 O.R. (2d) 721 at 727.
[16] [1966] 2 O.R. 37 at p. 42.

propriety which is sought to be preserved, making the decision is itself no less difficult. It is perhaps peculiar that in matters of law where the very nature of judicial decision-making involves a delicate balancing of competing interests, it should be determined in the abstract that one interest is necessarily paramount, independent of the circumstances of the particular case. Yet this is precisely what is called for when it is determined as an absolute rule that previous decisions, when indistinguishable and otherwise binding, must necessarily be followed. It places consistency higher than justice. An observation of Isaacs, J. made many years ago, comes to mind:

> "It is not, in my opinion, better that the Court should be persistently wrong than that it should be ultimately right."[17]

While equality, reliance, conceptual order and certainty are great virtues in the common law, they are not the only interests nor indeed are they necessarily paramount interests. Yet arguments propounding strict adherence to *stare decisis* must ultimately argue just that.

The concern that the question of adherence to *stare decisis* among intermediate appellate courts not be left to individual discretion may arise from a fear that because of the greater number of judges involved sitting in smaller panels hearing a great volume of cases, a proliferation of contradictory decisions may result which would indeed introduce uncertainty into the law. This very concern was advanced by at least two members of the House of Lords in *Davis v. Johnson*.[18] Better to leave it, so the argument goes, to the ultimate court of last resort to correct the error, because the risk there of introducing uncertainty into the law is minimal. Yet jurisdictions in which intermediate appellate courts do not observe strict application of the principle do not appear to be adversely affected, nor to suffer from a proliferation of contradictory decisions.[19]

Against the proponent of *stare decisis* who cites the need for certainty in the law, it has been argued that strict adherence to the rule often encourages courts to draw fine distinctions and expand recognized exceptions to the rule in order to avoid

---

[17] *Australian Agricultural Company et al. v. Federated Engine Drivers and Firemen's Association of Australasia* (1913), 17 C.L.R. 261 at p. 279.

[18] *Supra,* f.n. 5 per Lord Diplock at pp. 1137-8 and Lord Salmon at p. 1153.

[19] There has not, for example, been a great proliferation of contradictory decisions emanating from the Courts of Appeal in British Columbia or Manitoba. See the discussion *supra* at chap. 3 pages 40-43, 49-50.

previous decisions, in a manner which strains language and logic, thereby reducing the law to a state of greater uncertainty than if it had addressed the issue squarely and simply overruled the troublesome previous decision. A remark of Professor Friedmann, made with respect to the Supreme Court of Canada in the days when it still considered itself strictly bound by its previous decisions, well expresses this concern:

> But worse than the self-inflicted disability of the highest court to correct itself is the devious effect of forcing the highest as well as the lower courts into subterfuges. The many qualifications of stare decisis . . . provide some scope for judicial law reform. But the uncertainties as well as the inevitable hypocrisies of this method of evading rather than departing from precedent scarcely increase the respect for law. Neither do they give it that stability and certainty which is claimed from strict stare decisis.[20]

The Ontario Court of Appeal, constrained by its policy of strict adherence to *stare decisis*, is not entirely guiltless in this regard. It was earlier observed that in *Applebaum v. Gilchrist*[21] the Court of Appeal effectively overruled a troublesome previous decision through a somewhat tenuous distinction and by relying upon what would appear to have been an inconsequential change in a statute that was only of marginal relevance to the point in issue. Similarly, in *Weatherall v. Weatherall*[22] the court distinguished its previous decision so narrowly that a subsequent court faced with the same circumstances was able to come to the opposite conclusion. And again in *Maskewycz v. Maskewycz*[23] the court narrowly confined its previous, and by then outdated, decision by distinguishing it on grounds which appear to be irrelevant to the reasoning of the court in the earlier case.

Distinguishment in many ways has been the salvation of the common law, enabling it to respond effectively to changing social values. When engaged in legitimate use to prevent application of a principle beyond its logical scope it is an important and essential tool of logical reasoning and, therefore, judicial reasoning. But it is readily acknowledged that the mechanism has been used to restrict extension of unacceptable

---

[20] W. Friedmann, "*Stare Decisis* at Common Law Under the Civil Code of Quebec" (1953), 51 C.B. Rev. 723 at p. 748. A less critical but similar observation is made by Dickson, J. extrajudicially in "The Role and Function of Judges" *The Law Society of Upper Canada Gazette* (1980), Vol. XIV, 138 at p. 183.

[21] [1946] 4 D.L.R. 383.

[22] [1937] O.R. 572.

[23] (1973), 2 O.R. (2d) 713.

principles and indeed to narrow them to the point of emasculation. This appears to have been the exercise in *Weatherall v. Weatherall*[24] and *Maskewycz v. Maskewycz*[25], if not in *Applebaum v. Gilchrist*.[26] The practice has, to some extent, been applauded, if not endorsed. Extrajudicially, Dickson, J. has observed:

> Despite the limitations on creativity brought about by stare decisis, the law was not frozen. Principles from the previous century were not applied woodenly, as mere dead weight. By the genius of distinguishing facts the court escaped the folly of perpetuating to eternity, principles unsuited to modern circumstances. The seeming inflexibility implied by rigid adherence to precedent yielded to judicial innovation which purported to draw clever, if unconvincing, distinctions of fact in situations in which courts felt a precedent ought not to rule the affairs of parties before it.[27]

The observation was made as a comment upon the development and progression within the common law during the first half of this century despite a professed adherence to strict application of *stare decisis* which itself evolved during the latter part of the last century as a response to the philosophical attitudes of formalism and positivism then prevalent, no doubt inspired by a concern that the law be insulated from the vagaries of radical social and political change. But what justification can there be in the modern context for drawing "clever, if unconvincing, distinctions of fact" in order to preserve formal, but not conceptual adherence to *stare decisis*. The justification cannot be a concern for stability in the law in times of social and political instability if the matter is only of concern in respect of intermediate appellate courts. If strict application of *stare decisis* is a matter of form only, as it must be if distinguishment is exploited to the excesses that some of the recent cases illustrate, then uncertainty is indeed introduced; and that price is paid, it seems, for no reason other than the preservation of appearances.

Another argument against strict adherence to *stare decisis*, which, like the foregoing, takes as its base the need for intellectual honesty in the decision-making process, focuses on the technique of deferring to binding precedent in order to avoid

---

[24] *Supra*. f.n. 22.
[25] *Supra*, f.n. 23.
[26] *Supra*, f.n. 21.
[27] B. Dickson, "The Role and Function of Judges," *The Law Society of Upper Canada Gazette* (1980), Vol. XIV, p. 138 at p. 182.

the necessity of articulating reasons for rejecting a strongly competing position.

Laskin C.J.C. recently addressed the issue in his dissenting judgment in *Harrison v. Carswell*.[28] While it cannot be said that the majority judgment in that case avoided the issue there in question, it was held that a previous case was not distinguishable on any ground in law from a previous decision of the Court, the correctness of which was not questioned. The Chief Justice, however, was of the view that the former case was not determinative of the issue presently before the court and that so to hold, without more, was simply to decide without giving reasons for the decision. In reply to the question of whether the court "must pay mechanical deference to *stare decisis*", as he phrased it, the Chief Justice admonished:

> This Court, above all others in this country, cannot be simply mechanistic about previous decisions, whatever be the respect it would pay to such decisions. What we would be doing here, if we were to say that the *Peters* case, because it was so recently decided, has concluded the present case for us, would be to take merely one side of a debatable issue and say that it concludes the debate without the need to hear the other side.
>
> I do not have to call upon the pronouncements of members of this Court that we are free to depart from previous decisions in order to support the pressing need to examine the present case on its merits.
>
> . . . There should be, at least, some indication that the Court has addressed itself to the difficult issues that reside in the competing contentions that were made in this case. . . . What is important, however, is not whether we have a previous decision involving a 'brown horse' by which to judge a pending appeal involving a 'brown horse', but rather what were the principles and, indeed the facts, upon which the previous case, now urged as conclusive, was decided.[29]

The admonition is only collaterally related to the principle of *stare decisis*, but it is appropriate inasmuch as strict adherence to the principle may on occasion be exploited to permit the court to come to the result it would have reached in any event, but without being compelled to set forth the ground upon which it arrived at that conclusion. As the trend against a rigid application of the doctrine has gained force in recent years, it has become increasingly unacceptable under the contemporary perception of justice for a court simply to dismiss a strongly

---

[28] [1976] 2 S.C.R. 200.

[29] *Ibid.* at pp. 205-206.

controversial argument solely on the basis of precedent without dealing with the merits of the issue.

In both *Davis v. Johnson*[30] and *A.G. of St. Christopher v. Reynolds,*[31] in attempting to hold intermediate appellate courts to their previous decisions, the House of Lords suggested that since there is an appeal from those intermediate courts, they should follow their own decisions "and leave it to the final appellate tribunal to correct any error in law which may have crept into any previous decision."[32] The argument may have force in the British context but there are substantial arguments against its force in the Canadian context.

The predominant requirement in Canada of obtaining leave to appeal to the Supreme Court of Canada has increasingly rendered that Court inaccessible in all but the most important cases, and it by no means follows that ultimate court of last resort is necessarily available to correct error in the provincial courts of Appeal. Indeed, it would appear that in considering whether leave will be granted, the fact that the members of the courts of appeal. Indeed, it would appear that inconsidering below is by no means compelling.

The Supreme Court Act specifically deals with the general attributes necessary for leave to be granted: public importance, the importance of any issue of law or mixed law and fact, or of such a nature or significance as to warrant decision by the Supreme Court.[33] The practice of the court in dealing with leave applications indicates that "importance" must have general if not national or public significance. It appears that cases raising issues in particular areas of law which by their nature have a national dimension or are of general significance and importance throughout the country will be granted leave to some extent independent of the strength of the decision below,[34] while cases raising issues of purely local or regional significance, or matters unique to that province will not, even where the members of the court hearing the application disagree with the decision of the provincial appellate court below.[35]

No doubt this position is taken by the Supreme Court out of

---

[30] *Supra,* f.n. 5.

[31] [1979] 3 All E.R. 129.

[32] *Ibid.* at p. 140; see also *supra,* f.n. 5 at pp. 1137 and 1153.

[33] R.S.C. 1970, c. S-19, s-s 41(1).

[34] For example, constitutional law, administrative law, or construction of federal statutes of general or national significance and importance.

[35] See B. Laskin, "What Everyone Should Know About the Supreme Court of Canada" an address to the Empire Club, Toronto, March 12, 1981, at p. 10.

considered deference to the provincial appellate courts and in recognition of their position within the court structure; on matters of purely personal, local or regional importance, or unique importance within that province, or upon questions of construction of statutory provisions unique to that province, the provincial court of appeal, perhaps as a function of the federalist constitutional structure of Canada, is to be considered the court of last resort.

Independent of the legal qualifications for obtaining leave to appeal to the Supreme Court, the expense alone no doubt precludes the vast majority of litigants from proceeding beyond the level of the provincial court of appeal.[36] In this way as well, the so-called intermediate appellate court is effectively the court of last resort. A forceful argument therefore arises that as courts formally of last resort unanimously have found compelling the arguments against rigid adherence to *stare decisis,* intermediate appellate courts which are effectively courts of last resort in all but a miniscule number of cases, must equally be freed from the shackles of *stare decisis* in order that justice not be subordinated to precedent.

In examining the proper function of the principle of *stare decisis,* historical context should not be ignored. There can be no doubt that the principle is of fundamental importance to the common law system of justice. But the nature of its proper function within that system is a question to which there can be no certain answer; the answers offered will be as different as the times in which they are propounded. The matter is not static, but ever changing. What may have been of paramount importance in times of political instability when the 'rule of law' was just emerging, or in later times when mercantile and industrial development were seen to be the corner stones of society, may well not be of paramount importance today.

---

[36] Even the members of the House of Lords in *Davis v. Johnson* acknowledged this restriction and invited Parliament to act to make public funds available to overcome the problem; see Lord Salmon at p. 1153.

Index

modification of, 21, 22
termination of, 23, 24
peculiar position of, 20
Privy Council, refusal to follow, 24
variation by, effect on lower decision,
79

United States
  realism, effect of, 3, 4

Victoria Supreme Court
  foreign decisions overruled, effect, 81

Western Australia
  panel size, effect, 72